Praise for BEHIND THOSE EYES

"Lisa Whittle is a fresh voice [...] encouragement to her generation [...] able. She writes with effervescen[...] [...]ed insight. You will be blessed by *Behind Those Eyes*. Lisa lets you in behind her eyes . . . what you see will refresh and challenge you."

—JAN SILVIOUS, Speaker; and Author, *Big Girls Don't Whine* and *Smart Girls Think Twice*

"*Behind Those Eyes* is like an invitation to a fancy masquerade party. Lisa, as the hostess, invites each guest to consider the mask (Ms. Perfection, Ms. Happiness, and others) she has chosen to hide her insecurities and heartaches. Then Lisa gives each guest the best party favor: encouragement to consider removing her mask to allow the beauty of Jesus to radiate through the *real* woman behind the fancy mask. Lisa's message was a fresh reminder to me to resist the temptation to pick up my mask of Ms. Perfection."

—JACKIE KENDALL, National Speaker; Best-Selling Author; and President, Power to Grow Ministries

"Lisa Whittle shines a brilliant light into the games we play with ourselves—which become, then, the places where we doubt God and our own lovableness. She writes honestly, and she writes well. This book is a personal invitation to experience that Love, which of all loves, is the best."

—PAULA RINEHART, Author, *Strong Women, Soft Hearts* and *Better Than My Dreams*

"In an entertaining and articulate style, Lisa Whittle opens the way for a look inside ourselves to see the good, the bad, and the ugly roles we play as women. *Behind Those Eyes* exposes refreshing solutions and ways to find the hidden root of the roles we play to hide ourselves. Don't miss this opportunity to rise up and be your true self in Christ Jesus!"

—MARCIA RAMSLAND, The Organizing Pro;
International Speaker; and Author, *Simplify Your Life*,
Simplify Your Time, and *Simplify Your Space*

"Yes! Finally a book that doesn't try to teach me how to be the perfect Christian woman! Instead, it's a book that teaches me to embrace the reality that I'm truly an imperfect woman who serves a perfect God, and He thinks I'm pretty amazing just the way I am, warts and all! Thanks, Lisa. Every woman who struggles with *the great charade* needs to read this (and I think that includes us all!)."

—LESLIE NEASE, Women's Speaker and Writer, New Life 91.9
Radio Host, *Survivor: China* contestant, and Imperfect Wife and Mother

"It's not the shoes, not even the outfit . . . it's what's going on inside a woman that creates the facade of how she presents herself to others. In *Behind Those Eyes* Lisa Whittle gets to the heart of the matter, helping us acknowledge the fears and insecurities we feel. Her insight and encouragement to live honestly and transparently are refreshing gifts to us all."

—TAMMY MALTBY, Cohost, Aspiring Women; and
Author, *Confessions of a Good Christian Girl*

"In *Behind Those Eyes* Lisa Whittle offers an open invitation to truth-filled relationships. Taking a page from her own struggles for authenticity, Whittle writes with a fresh perspective on the impersonating roles we all fall into and why it is so hard for women just to be real. A message of courage and hope is found in this book, helpful to any woman trying to find out how to embrace her created self!"

—MARY KASSIAN, Author; Speaker; and Distinguished Professor
of Women's Studies, Southern Seminary

BEHIND THOSE EYES

What's *Really* Going on
Inside the Souls of Women

LISA WHITTLE

THOMAS NELSON
Since 1798

NASHVILLE DALLAS MEXICO CITY RIO DE JANEIRO BEIJING

Published in Nashville, Tennessee, by Thomas Nelson. Thomas Nelson is a trademark of Thomas Nelson, Inc.

Thomas Nelson, Inc. titles may be purchased in bulk for educational, business, fund-raising, or sales promotional use. For information, please e-mail SpecialMarkets@ThomasNelson.com.

Unless otherwise marked, Scripture quotations are taken from the Holy Bible: New International Version®. © 1973, 1978, 1984 by International Bible Society. Used by permission of Zondervan Publishing House. All rights reserved.

Scripture quotations marked NLT are taken from the Holy Bible, New Living Translation, © 1996. Used by permission of Tyndale House Publishers, Inc., Wheaton, IL 60189. All rights reserved.

Scripture quotations marked MSG are taken from *The Message* by Eugene H. Peterson. © 1993, 1994, 1995, 1996, 2000. Used by permission of NavPress Publishing Group. All rights reserved.

Scripture quotations marked NKJV are taken from the New King James Version®. © 1982 by Thomas Nelson, Inc. Used by permission. All rights reserved.

Scripture quotations marked TLB are taken from *The Living Bible*. © 1971. Used by permission of Tyndale House Publishers, Inc., Wheaton, Illinois 60189. All rights reserved.

Scripture quotations marked KJV are taken from the Holy Bible, King James Version.

Page Design by Casey Hooper

Library of Congress Cataloging-in-Publication Data

Whittle, Lisa.
  Behind those eyes : what's really going on inside the souls of women / Lisa Whittle.
      p. cm.
  Includes bibliographical references.
  ISBN 978-0-7852-2813-4 (pbk.)
  1. Christian women—Religious life. 2. Christian women—Conduct of life. I. Title.
BV4527.W498 2007
248.8'43—dc22

                                                                2007046474

Printed in the United States of America
08 09 10 11 RRD 5 4 3 2 1

To Colleen . . .

My best friend for life
and one of the most real people I know.
We were meant to journey together.
Definitely.

CONTENTS

CONTENTS

part three
THE REAL DEAL

ACKNOWLEDGMENTS

I marvel at how God put people in my path in order to allow this book to be born. It truly wouldn't have been possible without these key people in my life . . .

My support team of family and friends. The Reimers and the Whittles (two amazing families!), the Minors and the McGees (your friendship blesses Scotty and me more than you know), and our wonderful, thriving network of friends at Hickory Grove North—may we continue to "do life" together for many years to come.

My divinely connected new friend, Debbie Wickwire. I love how God led me to you, and I thank you for your open and discerning spirit, which allowed Him to guide you to believe in this project . . . and me.

My friends at Thomas Nelson Publishers. Thank you, Joey Paul, for seeing strength in this book and for your endorsement of it! And thanks to Jennifer Stair and Rhonda Hogan for your wise counsel and input. You women *rock*!

The women who inspired the stories in this book. I am becoming increasingly aware of how many gifted and wonderful women are out there who share my desire to "get real."

Thank you for your willingness to become vulnerable enough to share your stories in this book.

My three precious children: Graham, Micah, and Shae. You guys blow me away with your pure love for God. My greatest desire is that you feel the depth of His love toward you. Only He could love you more than Dad and me.

My husband and very cool life partner, Scotty. I praise God daily that He made you strong enough to handle this independent soul, and you do it with such mad love for me. (And lots of necessary humor!)

My heavenly Father, who never stops amazing me. Thank You for fixing everything in me that was ever broken. Please accept this book as my yes to You. You *are* my life.

part one

THE GREAT
CHARADE

one

THE TRUTH HURTS

What you're after is truth from the inside out.
—PSALM 51:6 MSG

It was the first time I remember being completely, brutally honest. I was six years old, and my friend Tina had invited me to attend a comedy show with her family one Friday night. Like any six-year-old, I was excited to get to go somewhere with someone besides my parents . . . even if I didn't quite understand what comedy was or where I was going. Going to the theater seemed such a grown-up thing to do, and I couldn't wait.

When the night arrived, Tina and her mom picked me up at my house. After a round of hugs and kisses from my parents, we were on our way. The ride to the theater was filled with giggles from the backseat as Tina and I chatted away about the flavors of our new lip glosses and showed each other our sparkly shoelaces . . . things of monumental importance to six-year-old girls. The drive was short, and we arrived in the theater just as the show was starting. I settled into my padded seat on the front row of the auditorium, with Tina on my right side and a complete stranger—a man in his midforties—on my left.

The curtain parted and the performers took their place. They did a few silly things, a few entertaining things, and a few things I didn't quite understand. Little did I know that in a matter of moments, the opening illustration for this book would be born out of a hugely embarrassing moment in my young life.

We watched a comedian perform a short stand-up comedy routine. I didn't know what a standup routine was at the time, but I did know that the guy onstage was only a little funny, and I was getting bored. I started to squirm. I was just about to ask Tina's mom if I could be excused to go to the restroom when I heard the man onstage engage the audience with a question. "Will you do me a favor?" he asked. My little six-year-old self perked up. I had my best listening ears on, waiting for the asked favor, ready for action. "Look beside you, on either side. If the person sitting next to you is ugly, please stand up." *What a strange favor to ask*, I thought.

I looked to my right and saw my friend Tina. She was a beautiful, petite girl who was anything but ugly. No luck there. I turned my head to the other side to glance at the man sitting to my left. When I did, he looked at me with a horrified expression as if anticipating what I might do. His fears were warranted. Without hesitation, I sprang to my feet to bear witness to the fact that the man had been a little less than blessed, genetically speaking.

Since I was on the front row, my actions were hard to ignore. The crowd roared with laughter at the sight of a little girl in her most honest state, standing to her feet at the bogus request of a man with a microphone. I turned around to see that no one else was standing, and although I barely knew what a joke was, I quickly realized that the joke was on me. I sat down as fast as I could, wishing I had never stood. But the damage was already done.

OUR NEED FOR AUTHENTICITY

Many years later, I am still both horrified and humored by this true story. It is hard for me to tell it without cringing at my willingness to spill the beans about the looks of a stranger sitting beside me! But I have come to realize that such is the innocence and honesty of children. And although they don't quite understand how to tactfully handle their honesty yet, bless them for their lack of pretense.

This is the kind of gut-level honesty that only pure-hearted children can truly provide—the type of unedited truth that you appreciate on one hand and that crushes you like a can in a recycling bin on the other. These are statements from children like, "Mommy, why is your tummy so squishy?" Or, "Eww . . . your breath stinks." Ouch. The truth hurts.

While such statements are painful enough coming from your own children, they are a bit harder to explain away when made to strangers. Like the time you take your precious child to the media store in the mall where a teenager struggling with acne is ringing up your purchases, and you hear a little voice behind you say, "Sorry you have the chicken pox." Gulp. Since the powers to become invisible have already been checked out that day by one of the Fantastic Four, you grab your purchase, mumble a halfhearted thanks, and slink away. No save there.

> Rudeness is never called for. But a little more honesty in the world might not hurt either.

Though you can get away with this kind of honesty when you are an innocent three-year-old, it is not recommended to try this level of candor in your Monday night Bunco group. Fortunately, most of us have enough manners to not intentionally offend someone by a hurtful comment. Please understand me. Rudeness is never called for. But a little more honesty in the world might not hurt either.

Perhaps the better word for what I'm trying to say is *authenticity* . . . being genuine, transparent, and real with one another. Of all the many shortcomings I have, I do not struggle often with saying what I feel. (Sometimes that is the problem!) I tend to be honest, if not a bit blunt sometimes.

I seek authenticity in my life, though I don't always achieve it. And I cannot swallow pretense in any capacity. You know, the kind of pretense you sometimes feel from others and even sense yourself portraying in certain situations.

TALKING ABOUT NOTHING

I had one of these moments not long ago during a visit to my hair salon. Now, anyone who really knows me knows that I am a girly-girl. I love to have my nails done and think heaven must be something like a day spa. But with three young children and a busy life, I have to settle for my scheduled eight-week hair appointments. After all, the hair salon is a place I enjoy visiting. I admit: I am a sucker for the relaxing atmosphere in upscale salons . . . the bittersweet smell of hair products . . . the tranquil melodies piped throughout the room. I go to a place where the stylists are called *artistic directors*, and most of them sport funky haircuts, multiple piercings, and trendy attire. I have bought into the high-priced haircut, and my husband graciously indulges me by agreeing to pay the ridiculous cost to make me feel beautiful. And I usually enjoy it but not on this day.

After my initial meet-and-greet with my stylist, I was introduced to Bree, a cute girl with a retro haircut who would be my colorist for the day. I welcomed her presence as my grays were beginning to multiply and could no longer be plucked out with my tweezers.

"Hi," Bree said. "How are you today?" I felt compelled, if not obligated, to engage in conversation with her. "Fine, thanks," I responded. "How about you?" "Good . . . good. Can't complain," she said.

Since casual conversation was not really of interest to me at that particular moment, I looked down at the magazine I brought with me in the hopes that I might actually get to read an article or two before Bree was through with my hair. But she wasn't picking up on my vibe very well. "Do you have children?" she asked, clearly only halfway interested. "Yes. I have three," I answered. "Oh, wow," she said. "You must be really busy." *More than you know*, I thought. "Yeah, pretty much," I replied. I knew I had to ask: "How about you? Any kids?" "One little boy," Bree said.

At this point I noticed that we were talking *at* each other in short sentences, which made things a bit awkward, almost forced. "Oh. Boys are great, aren't they?" I volleyed back to her. "Yeah, they are," she said. "Where do your kids go to school?" "It's a private Christian school. Do you live on this side of town?" I asked. She explained to me where she lived, and a few more expected questions followed.

At this point in our extremely stale and mechanical conversation, I started to become irritated. The kind of irritated where you want to literally jump out of your skin. The feeling you get when the guy behind you in the movies is talking too loudly. I was annoyed. And it wasn't about wanting to read my magazine; I had long forgotten that I had even brought it with me. No, it was about something else entirely.

In that moment, I realized that Bree and I were talking about *nothing*.

Nothing at all. At least nothing that really mattered. Oh, we were having a conversation. We were playing verbal volleyball with our words, talking about topics—topics that held some marginally important elements but were still just topics. We were settling for a generic conversation that wouldn't matter in about two seconds. And it irritated me.

Suddenly I had an overwhelming desire to stop Bree in her foiling process, spin my chair around to look at her, and ask, "What are we talking about? What is the point to this conversation? What's going on in your life right now? What is Bree really all about?" I knew that hidden behind those warm hazel eyes, a story was waiting to emerge.

But that would have been too intrusive . . . too personal for a couple of women who had just met and had a comfortable contractual relationship going on. And the sad reality was that on that day, I wasn't willing for Bree to share more with me than what I had bargained for. It was far easier to impersonate a put-together mom with money to burn on a mod haircut than to share my heart with her. So I chose to settle for this boring interaction between us. Bree and I were both in full-on *female impersonation* mode.

FEMALES IMPERSONATING . . . *FEMALES?*

In 2000, our family moved to a beautiful home outside of Nashville. We were excited by the promise of a new job in a new city, though the area was unfamiliar to us. With the moving truck still parked in front of our house, I started unpacking boxes. In assembly-line fashion and with much fervor, I was able to accomplish quite a bit while the children were occupied by their visiting grandparents. Boxes were piling up in the garage, and the neighbors were beginning to notice that the new kids on the block had, indeed, arrived.

Brringg. Somehow, over the noise of my chattering children, I heard the doorbell ring. Buried in boxes, I called out to my mother in the front room. "Hey, Mom! Can you get the door?" My mother obliged, and I could hear a muffled conversation on the porch. A few moments later, my mother found me in the kitchen, amid bubble wrap and crumpled newspaper. She had a funny grin on her face, which piqued my attention and caused me to pause my manic unpacking. "Who was it?" I asked. She playfully quipped, "Dolly Parton is at the door. She wants to know if she can have some of your boxes." I could tell by her tone that the real Dolly Parton was not at the door, but whoever it was would surely be worth going to see!

I quickly made my way to the front door, which my mom had left half-open. Even from across the room, I could see the signature bright lipstick, yellow-blonde hair, and mascara-

laden eyes. Mom was right . . . Dolly Parton *was* at my door
. . . or, at least, someone who looked just like her! "Hello,"
the mystery woman said. "I see you just moved in and have
quite a few boxes in your garage. I live in the house across
the street, and I'm just moving out. Could I take some of
those boxes off your hands for you?"

I didn't care who she was; I just wanted to get rid of the
boxes and get back to my unpacking. "Sure," I said. "Have at
them!" With that, the mystery woman—who looked very
much like Dolly Parton—gave a big smile and offered a
"Thanks!" as she headed toward the garage.

A few days later and still curious about the box taker, I
went looking for answers. I asked around and found out from
neighbors that the mystery woman
resembling Dolly Parton was actually her sister. It certainly made
sense; the family resemblance was
uncanny. I have to admit, though,
that my first thought was not that
the woman might be Dolly's sister.
I suspected, as a naive newcomer
to Music City USA, that I had en-
countered my first real-life female impersonator in the form of
a fake Dolly Parton. I was close, but I was still wrong in my
assumptions.

> We, as women, often lead others to believe we are someone other than who we really are. The story behind our eyes often goes untold.

This story has great relevance in this chapter about truth
and authenticity. Just as I was led by my eyes to believe that
the woman standing at my door was someone other than who
she really was, so we, as women, often lead others to believe
we are someone other than who we really are.

The story behind our eyes often goes untold. Our engaging smiles mask things we don't want others to know about us. We cover our weaknesses and heartaches with immaculately groomed clothes and manufactured conversations. We impersonate the females we *want* to be—carefree, fun loving, deeply spiritual, genuinely caring, supportive, capable, strong, assertive, put together, and ridiculously happy—rather than the women we really are.

In fact, what is really going on inside our souls is so cavernous that we fear anyone who enters its depths would never again see the light of day. So we put up the barricades, allowing very few to penetrate the walls we've erected around us as a means of self-protection. Since we are genetically descendants of Eve, we don't need to alter our outward appearance to impersonate a real DNA-born female. But we often alter our personalities to fit a role we think we need to play, which certainly holds the same pretense.

> This is the great charade of womanhood, and most of us have gotten really good at it.

The truth is that most females usually know when we get into this impersonation mode. We've perfected the fake laugh and the token smile . . . both worthy of an Oscar. We feign interest in topics that are not interesting to us and are determined to maintain our images to the bitter end. We desperately hope and believe that someone, somewhere, somehow, will think we have our lives figured out and perfected to a T.

This is the great charade of womanhood, and most of us have gotten really good at it.

Why do we do it? We lack honesty and authenticity, and our past experiences lead us to believe it is in our best interests to keep our true feelings hidden.

NOT ALL BAD

All of us are faced with truths at one point in our life. And truths are good to know because they often spur us on to action. Take, for instance, *American Idol*, the megahit TV singing competition that turns unknown singers into household names. Thousands of people all across America wait in line for hours and in all kinds of weather to get their shot at fame by auditioning for this show, hoping to be selected to compete in Hollywood.

For TV viewers, one of the most entertaining aspects of this show is the auditions, with hours of footage of people singing off-key, dancing ridiculously, insulting the judges, and making fools of themselves. We love it when hard-nosed British judge Simon Cowell weighs in with his point-blank, no-holds-barred comments: "It was really terrible . . . dreadful . . . awful . . . a waste of time . . . pointless. You have no talent. You can't sing. You are embarrassing yourself." To be fair, Simon is usually saying what most people are thinking, though perhaps he expresses it a bit more rudely than most of us would. But he is telling the truth to these people. And the truth may hurt, but the truth may also send these aspiring stars directly into singing lessons. Or better yet, perhaps that truth leads them to another career path altogether . . . one they are actually qualified for. Either way, the truth, as told by the judges of these aspiring singers, spurs them on to some kind of action.

Although I have never had the desire (or talent) to try out for *American Idol*, I have also had my own reality checks from time to time. Like the time in middle school a female classmate looked at me in gym class and informed me that I needed to do a better job of shaving my armpits. Okay, so she could have said it in the privacy of the locker room rather than in front of my male and female peers, but still, it was the truth. And at that moment, the truth really hurt.

Or the time in high school that my tenth-grade crush looked at me from across the desk and said, "I just noticed something . . . you have a bigger mustache than I do!" Yet again, the truth according to my high school crush was, in fact, true. But boy, did it hurt to hear about it. Ultimately, these once-painful comments were good truths to know since they jump-started my lifelong routine of shaving and waxing. They spurred me on to action and kept me from inevitable future hurtful comments that were sure to come had I not responded.

> A painful truth revealed to us can also be the catalyst for us to become a mere shell of who we really are beneath all of the fluff.

In the same way, sometimes truths about our inner selves hurt to the point where we also want to make a change. Many people have determined not to become alcoholics or drug abusers because their parents were. Others have stopped the cycle of physical, emotional, or even sexual abuse by refusing to inflict pain on those vulnerable to them, though they once suffered themselves at the hands of an abuser. Those are life truths that, when realized, have resulted in positive actions. But a painful truth revealed to us can also be the catalyst for us to become a mere shell of who we really are beneath all of the fluff.

I remember taking a back-lot tour of some popular TV sets during my vacation to Disney's MGM Studios one year. Our group rode on a guide-driven tram through lots that once housed such hit shows as *The Golden Girls* and *Leave It to Beaver*. I was amazed by the immaculate and beautiful yards; the houses looked very inviting from the outside. Just seeing them took me back to some of my favorite shows and made me want to open the door and enter into what looked like such a welcome place.

But a funny thing happened when we drove around to the back of the homes. The interior consisted of exposed beams and empty spaces representing rooms; they looked nothing like the picture of togetherness we had seen from the front. The fully occupied, fully operating homes presented to us were nothing but facades with a good paint job and professionally maintained landscaping. Sound familiar?

BORN PRETENDERS

My older son, Graham, was born with a desire for a costume change. That is, from a very early age, he was fascinated by various TV and movie characters, and he often emulated them by taking on their personas, either in a costume or in role-playing. He loved to pretend and could be quite inventive with his pillowcase capes (think superheroes), scarf headbands (think ninjas), and keen sense of imagination.

One day, in the middle of a game of role-playing, five-year-old Graham suddenly became quiet. He walked up to me and deadpanned, "Mom, I simply cannot continue to pretend to be someone I am not." And then he turned around and walked away to resume playing.

I didn't mean to laugh at his precious moment of stanch seriousness, but I could barely hold it in. His naive statement was quite humorous, considering that I had watched him for most of his life pretend to be someone he was not, even just three minutes beforehand! And his childish conviction only lasted about a minute, since he had resumed his game of pretend. Graham was quite literally a born pretender, as so many of us are.

You can't really blame us for pretending to be someone we are not. We are somewhat geared this way. From a very early age, we pretend to be singers, beauty queens, pop stars, princesses, brides, and mommies. Malls now house retail shops that allow girls as young as three years old to have their hair and makeup professionally done. These stores have become wildly popular birthday party places, and young girls absolutely love them. The moms don't help with this either. We love to see our little angels all dolled up with glitter in their hair, a sparkly tiara, or a pop-star headset, pretending right alongside them that they are the beauty queens they look like.

I still remember a time as a child being so embarrassed by my dad seeing me pretend. I must have been about eight years old, and I had just arrived home from school with my mother. Impulsively, after getting out to get the mail, I jumped onto the trunk of the car (picture a very long vehicle with large trunk . . . this was the 1970s) and began to do the *pageant wave* I had seen pageant winners do on TV. I was pretending to be the exuberant new winner of a crown, and I was doing my best wave to my adoring audience looking on. My father, who was home early that day, surprised me when he came out of the house just in time to see me. Humored by what he saw, he grinned widely and said, "I see you, Lisa girl." I was so embarrassed. After all, I hadn't wanted anyone to see me pretending to be someone I wasn't. It's as if I knew even at that young age that it was a silly thing to do.

To be fair, many of us do not go into life wanting to be pretenders, but we have at some point embraced the idea when it suited our desires. Think back to one of the best pretenders of all time in the Bible: Judas Iscariot. Mark 14 tells the story of Judas's hypocrisy, deception, and betrayal of Jesus. Judas was chosen by Jesus to be one of the twelve disciples, yet he disowned his position for money and power when the opportunity arose. Judas pretended to be a sold-out follower of Jesus Christ, but he was, in fact, a sellout. He made the money he craved by outing Jesus to the officials who were looking to arrest and kill Him, and he did it in the cruelest of ways: he planted a kiss on the Master's cheek. Judas pretended to love Jesus, but in fact, he loved no one but himself.

Judas is not the only one who has staged a cover-up. Remember Gary Ridgway, the infamous Green River Killer? This Washington man, who confessed to killing forty-eight women (though the number of victims is said to be even higher), lived a successful double life as a doting husband and dutiful dad while carrying out his violent murder spree. He was one of the most notorious serial killers in history, yet his wife of fourteen years had no knowledge of his murderous side. Ridgway covered his tracks well and successfully fooled those from whom he wanted to keep the truth hidden.

> Many of us do not go into life wanting to be pretenders, but we have at some point embraced the idea when it suited our desires.

Many modern-day examples of cover-ups can be seen in movies. Like the movie where a girl went undercover as a boy in order to report a story for the high school paper from a male perspective. Or the movie where a white male transformed himself into a black male in order to obtain a university scholarship only offered to African American students. Or the movie where a father was denied access to his children and the only way to see them was to disguise himself and pretend he was a female nanny. All of these acts of cinematic pretense hold the same motive as we often do when we pretend to be someone we are not: these cover-ups meet a need at the time to get us more of what we want when we do not believe the truth will.

SOUL CRAVINGS

Make no mistake about it: women are yearning for something real. We're hungry for truth and authenticity. We crave honesty. We want someone to cut through the fluff and get to the bottom line. Dr. Phil—popular psychologist turned TV host—made his mark by becoming the tell-it-like-it-is voice of the new millennium. His success has been fueled by not only his good counsel and his ease with his audience but also his willingness to expose truths to his guests that others might not be as eager to reveal for fear of rejection or backlash.

John Eldredge, in his book *The Sacred Romance*, has this to say about our cravings for something real:

> In one of the greatest invitations ever offered to man, Christ stood up amid the crowds in Jerusalem and said, "If anyone is thirsty, let him come to me and drink. Whoever believes in me, as the Scripture has said, streams of living water will flow from within him" (John 7:37–38). If we aren't aware of our soul's deep thirst, his offer means nothing. But, if we

will recall, it was from the longing of our hearts that most of us first responded to Jesus. Somehow, years later, we assume he no longer calls to us through the thirst of our heart.[1]

King Solomon, known as the wisest man in his day, gave a beautiful analogy in the book of Proverbs: "It is good for workers to have an appetite; an empty stomach drives them on" (16:26 NLT). His words perfectly illustrate how we crave God. When our facades fail and our quick fixes don't solve anything in the end, our appetite for something more sends us straight into the loving arms of Jesus Christ. And He is the only One who ever truly satisfies us.

Women, our craving for chocolate is nothing in comparison to our craving for love. Our craving for water after a sweaty workout is nothing in comparison to our craving for genuine acceptance. We want someone to say he loves us and truly mean it. We want someone to know us from the inside out, warts and all, and not think twice about our many flaws. We want unconditional love. We desire to find purpose. We seek attention, and we crave acceptance.

> Our appetite for something more sends us straight into the loving arms of Jesus Christ. And He is the only One who ever truly satisfies us.

Desperately Seeking Susan, starring pop icon Madonna, was a popular movie in the 1980s. In this movie, a bored housewife named Roberta follows the progress of an anonymous woman she knows only by the name of Susan, who regularly places ads in the personals for her boyfriend, Jim. In one such personal ad, Roberta finds out that the couple is going to be meeting in New York. Out of curiosity, Roberta goes to New York to see them. In the process, she winds up obtaining Susan's coat and finds a locker key in the pocket of the jacket. Roberta then places her own personal ad for Susan to meet with her so she can return the key to her. Through a string of unfortunate circumstances, Roberta then takes on the identity of Susan, and things begin to get complicated.

It's a silly movie with a far-fetched plot, but it is a movie I have never forgotten. It reminds me of something in my life to which I can relate.

I just may be the real-life version of Roberta, and so may you. The real-life Roberta is doing some desperate seeking of her own. She's not looking for Susan . . . even though she may think she is. She may think her Susan needs a man to take care of her. Her Susan may be the career she thinks she needs to find significance in the eyes of others. She may be looking for a Susan who will be the answer to all her questions of why from her past and what could have been in her future.

But in truth, the real-life Roberta's looking goes way beyond what a personal ad can yield her, no matter who or what is on the other end. She is searching for a pillow soft enough to lay her head on at night. She is long-ing for a blanket thick enough to melt the parts of her heart that have frozen solid over time. She is craving something so much that she would gladly publish a full-page ad to find it. But until she finds it, she will have to be currently satisfied with looking perfect, appearing happy, portraying confidence, and sound-ing spiritual to make her feel better and get more people to love her. And she's not the only one who is. Let me be the

> The truth may initially hurt, but the truth may be the best thing that has ever happened to you.

first one to fall in line after her as I have at times been guilty of the same.

In the next four chapters, I will introduce you to some characters you may already be very familiar with since they are the roles we often play to impersonate the women we want to be—or, at least, the women we want others to think we are. As you read, see if you find yourself in the characters of Ms. Perfection, Ms. Happiness, Ms. Confidence, or Ms. Spirituality. And keep in mind, if you do, that the truth may initially hurt, but the truth may be the best thing that has ever happened to you.

two

MS. PERFECTION

To all perfection I see a limit;
but your commands are boundless.

—PSALM 119:96

I call it the Great Sunday Morning Fakeout. In fact, it is so wide-spread, I believe it should be an actual syndrome, and possibly an epidemic. Those of you churchgoing women, say a big *amen.* You know what I'm talking about.

Here's the scenario. Somewhere in the United States, a well-intentioned family is getting ready for Sunday morning church. The crew is usually headed up by Mom, who has been out of bed far longer than she should have been and has guzzled far more coffee than she should have had. She is already on edge as she anticipates the circuslike atmosphere she is sure to face. After a quick breakfast of Pop Tarts and juice boxes, she heads to the bathroom to ready herself. Upon her fourth interruption, she forgoes her own readying and proceeds to prepare the rest of the crew. Her presence is met with resistance, if not hostility, as the crew does not desire major overhaul yet this morning. But the crew leader sticks to task, keeping the goal in mind. The fakeout is all too important.

For the next half hour, Mom becomes fashion director, hair stylist, ringmaster, and even psychologist to her brood, with some help from dear old Dad (if she's lucky). Along the way, she has to stop to wipe tears, smooth tangles, and change clothes smeared with Pop Tart filling. She has to flex in her original wardrobe choices upon finding out that Junior no longer likes horizontal stripes on his shirt, just vertical ones. The preparation is almost complete. But it is not without incident.

She hears her younger son call out, "Mom? Where are you? Can you come here for a second?" An inner struggle ensues. *Should I, or shouldn't I?* Deciding to momentarily ignore her beloved child, she quickly brushes her teeth. With no second requests coming in, she heads for the shower. She is almost there when she hears a squeal coming from the hallway. She rushes down the hall to be greeted by her toddler, her beautiful white dress soaking wet, standing over a puddle on the floor. "Uh-oh, Mommy," she says, her big eyes filling with tears.

Delegating the task of cleanup to her husband, Mom hurries to the bathroom to finally see about herself. After a quick makeup application, she is in good-enough shape to leave the house. In truth, she is glad to have gotten clothes on her body, since the ones she tried on originally would not quite zip.

Dad has taken the cue and is loading the crew into the car. Mom hops in with an armful of bags and Bibles, nearly out of breath. They are off to church.

Halfway down the street, a sweet voice from the back of the car asks, "Mommy, can I have my juice?" The crew chief looks around the car to see that she has forgotten an all-important detail: no juice cup. "Oh, baby, I'm sorry. Mommy forgot it. We'll be there in a few minutes, and you can get some juice in Sunday school, okay?" The toddler isn't taking the news well. Being without her juice is absolutely unbearable. She starts to wail with the intensity of a siren on the way to put out a fire. Tears burst out of her little eyes. After all, this is the thirstiest morning of her life. She has never, ever been thirstier. If only Mommy had known!

As in most moments of stress, a small issue quickly escalates into a slightly larger one. "Yeah, Mom, and Brother took my favorite toy and won't give it back." Brother doth protest. "I did not!" he screams. "Yes, you did. And I can prove it!" The two bear cubs are now fighting, full force.

The car is filled with the sounds of verbal sparring and high-pitched wailing. "Knock it off!" warns Dad. Hearing his voice reminds Mom that there is something they need to discuss. "I really wish you wouldn't cut the grass so short anymore, honey. It looks pretty bad and is starting to die." Flabbergasted that she has chosen this moment to discuss horticulture, the usually cool dad looks at her and says sarcastically, "Great. Thanks for the tip. The next time you get the urge to get outside and cut the grass, just let me know. Todd's wife cuts their grass, and I don't see why you couldn't do that. You stay home all day. What else do you do?" Oh, man. Those are fighting words.

On a scale from slightly annoyed to overtly angry, Mom and Dad are off the charts. It has been quite a morning. They spend the next ten minutes riding to church in stony silence.

The rest of the crew knows better than to talk right now. After all, they are all alumni of the Great Sunday Morning Fakeout. Been there, done that, got the T-shirt.

The family arrives at church to a full parking lot with no open spaces. With no option than to keep looking, they circle the parking spaces like a shark to its prey. Ten more minutes pass before they find a spot for their vehicle. "Everybody out!" snaps Dad. The crew obliges, but not without incident.

"Where are we going for lunch?" asks the older son. Mom responds, "We don't know yet. Please don't ask us that right now, okay?" The younger son pipes in. "I hope it's not that Mexican place again. I don't like the rice. I hate that place!" The older son answers back, "I love that place. You only like dumb places like that hamburger place with the gross fries. We better not be going there!"

"Stop it!" hisses Mom. "We're almost inside the church." The fakeout is already under way. Pasting on their smiles, the happy party of five greets the men waiting at the double doors. "Good morning!" The cheery sound of Mom's voice surprises even herself. The boys turn around abruptly to see where their mom went. Assured that she is still there and just had a major voiceover, they turn back around to high-five the greeters while the toddler in Daddy's arms flashes a big, toothy smile. They have learned from the best.

> I can easily write about this impersonation of perfection because like most women I know, I have taken part in it.

After shuffling the kids to their classes, Mom and Dad collapse into their seats in the already-full worship center. They breathe a collective sigh of relief, for though in this short morning they have lost something, found something, argued over something, and resolved nothing, the Great Sunday Morning Fakeout has once again proven successful. The mission to portray a perfect family going to church was effectively accomplished.

I would like to tell you that this scenario was based on market research. But the truth is that I can easily write about this impersonation of perfection because like most women I know, I have taken part in it.

As a matter of fact, I took part in a Great Sunday Morning Fakeout of my own not long ago. It was Easter Sunday of last year to be exact—a day primed and ready for fakeouts all across the country. And so it was with me on that day.

My children at the time were ages eight, six, and four. Although the oldest two are boys and are no longer willing to wear matching clothes, they still allow me to dress all three of them in coordinating colors. This Easter, I took particular care in picking out just the right suits, shirts, and shoes for the boys to go with the bright plaid dress my daughter was to wear. As I am sure most people know, the unspoken rule about Easter attire is that the female outfit takes precedence over the male outfit. (Women from the South know this, especially.) So the color scheme of green was built around a size 4 toddler dress for our little Easter princess.

In my quest to find perfect outfits for the children, I had nearly forgotten to shop for myself. While some years I simply wore an existing outfit on Easter Sunday, this year I was determined to get something new. *I don't have anything green*, I reasoned.

With the day looming closer, I managed to make a quick trip to the mall without the children in tow. I tried on quite a few things until finally I found just the right skirt and matching shirt-sweater combination. I quickly purchased it and headed home.

Easter Sunday came, along with the usual morning rush. After getting the children dressed, I consulted with my husband on his outfit and got dressed in my own. I was pleased with my green patterned shirt, beautiful green sweater, and bright, white skirt. I was starched and ready.

We took a few pictures, loaded up the car, and left for church. To my delight, things were running rather smoothly for a Sunday morning. We arrived at the church and entered the sanctuary. Our pastor had encouraged us to bring our entire families to the service with us, which we had decided to do. We greeted my parents inside and took our seats on a row midway up. While the children drew pictures and worked puzzles, the adults worshiped. The music was uplifting, the sermon was inspiring, and we looked just perfect. Things couldn't have been better.

About halfway through the service, I looked down at my crisp, clean white linen skirt. That's when I noticed a glaring flaw in the plan. Right down the middle of my skirt, stretching from my left side to my right, was a bright, royal blue pen mark smiling back at me. Horrified at what I saw, I realized the only way to remove the stain was to take it to the dry cleaners. I couldn't believe that after all my stressing and striving, the look I wanted to achieve that Easter morning was ruined with a mark from my son's pen. *So much for perfection*, I thought.

I learned a great lesson from that simple story. It was as if God said to me, *Lisa, you can prepare and plan and anticipate things and seek perfection. But just in case you have forgotten that you are anything but perfect, let this remind you of just that.* The pen mark symbolized to me the imperfections in my life, no matter how well thought out and organized I may be.

Women, the truth is that God doesn't have to prove anything to us to let us see our imperfections. We can manage that all on our own. As 2 Corinthians 3:5 tells us, "Not that we are competent in ourselves to claim anything for ourselves." It doesn't take us very long to see and know that in our flesh, perfection is not even remotely possible.

But while it is not possible to achieve on this earth, perfection is, perhaps, the most common characteristic that women impersonate. We get caught up in the trap of trying to appear perfect to others. Society sells us pictures and symbols of perfection in the news media, print ads, and gossip magazines. They have pitched us an image . . . and we've fallen for it. We are buying into the notion of perfect wife, perfect mother, and perfect package, at the expense of ourselves and our loved ones.

> God doesn't have to prove anything to us to let us see our imperfections. We can manage that all on our own.

THE PERFECT WIFE SYNDROME

"Hello," she says, in her perfect, melodic voice. Her perfectly manicured hands open widely. "Welcome to Stepford." Stepford's resident realtor, Mrs. Wellington, greets the new couple in town, Walter and Joanna, just as she has the others. A perfect greeting by Ms. Perfection herself.

In the first few minutes of watching the movie *The*

Stepford Wives, I knew I wouldn't last until the ending credits. It is, after all, a remake of the classic—a strange, silly spoof of the original. Or so I've heard. And while the movie itself did not hold my attention, I was intrigued by the idea behind it: women with good minds and hearts being traded in for newer, more perfect models of themselves to serve as more perfect wives to their husbands. I began to wonder, *Is this what we are doing as wives? Are we trying to be the perfect Barbie for our Ken in the hopes that he will love us more . . . or, at the very least, that people will think he does? Who are we trying to fool, anyway?*

I have to confess, I would love for someone else to write this part of the chapter. My feelings of inadequacy as a wife are sure to come out as I share my heart with you; being a wife is one of the most difficult tasks I have ever undertaken. It is a tough job as those of us who are married know.

It's not that the job itself is all that hard. I mean it sincerely when I say that it can truly be such a blessing to be someone's wife—if that is, in fact, your life situation. The partnership between husband and wife can be fantastic. The friendship between spouses is meant to be very unique and special. However, many of us are far too busy impersonating good marriages to actually *have* good marriages. We are hoping to impress others by making them think we are perfect wives. And only our hair stylist and our husband know any different.

Appearances of perfection can be deceiving, especially when it comes to marriage. I experienced this several years ago. Our family was going through a difficult time—my husband, Scotty, had lost his job and as a result, finances were running low, emotions were running high, and we were struggling to cope with life. Feeling inadequate and intimidated, I began to notice that everyone around me seemed more perfect than they did before. This perception only made me feel worse.

One particular Sunday, we were in church, and the pastor was preaching on marriage. Though Scotty and I were doing okay in our marriage at the time, we had also had better times in our married life. Things were definitely not as good as they could be. During the sermon, I noticed a very well-dressed, sharp-looking couple who, by all appearances, really had it together. They were sitting with their well-groomed children between them on the pew in front of us, and they looked to me to be very close and in love. When the pastor made a point, they would glance at each other in a kind way, and after the sermon was over, they embraced before they walked out. *How nice*, I thought. *That couple really has it all.*

On the way home, I asked my husband if he knew the people sitting in front of us. He said that he did and that the man was in his weekly Bible study. I waited, fully expecting him to then tell me about the man's good job and the wife's community involvement and the children's accomplishments. But instead, he said something entirely different. He told me that we really needed to pray for them because they were in a sad situation . . . on the brink of divorce because of the husband's infidelity and the wife's bout with severe depression. *Divorce? Depression?* I thought. *Not that perfect couple!* I felt sure my husband had mistaken the couple I had seen for a different couple.

I began to describe the man and woman to him, to make

> Appearances of perfection can be deceiving, especially when it comes to marriage.

sure he understood exactly who I was talking about. After matching up details, he assured me that the people I had seen were, in fact, the same people he knew from the Bible study. I was floored! I had been deceived by my own perceptions of perfection. I determined then that I would no longer judge the happiness of anyone based upon how well they groom themselves because the truth is most of us clean up rather well when we want to. But none of us is a perfect wife, and none of us has a perfect marriage.

Since most of us have never actually seen a perfect wife, would we even know what one looks like? While not completely the Stepford model, here's what I envision . . .

She looks amazing. Her hair, nails, skin, teeth, and body are in fantastic condition, since she knows that her husband is physiologically prewired toward sight. She is a gracious hostess to her husband at all times, providing him with the comforts and conveniences every man needs and desires from his partner . . . and she does so without a trace of resentment or pride. She laughs at her husband's jokes. She encourages him without sounding preachy. And she looks at him with the longing of a schoolgirl to her first crush.

> Most of us clean up rather well when we want to. But none of us is a perfect wife, and none of us has a perfect marriage.

She cooks for him and cleans for him. She is the most exciting and adventurous lovemaking partner he has ever had or will hope to have. She rocks his world, and he loves her for it. She prays for him fervently, loves him passionately, and honors him completely. She is the personification of perfection in a marriage. And she intimidates me to death.

This is my husband's dream girl. (And if I may so boldly suggest . . . your husband's too.) To be fair, many women try to be our husband's ideal mate, at least on some level. Most of us do try to do at least some of these things. We get books like *1001 Ways to Keep Your Husband Interested in You*. We use Crest Whitestrips. We make his favorite cake to surprise him . . . every blue moon. We try to exercise at least once a month, and we pray a lot about exercising grace toward him.

Ladies, we act like a perfect wife more than we actually are one. If our husbands are predisposed toward good looks and good sex, our predisposition is toward recruiting and reworking our future mates until they resemble some form of their former selves, albeit with major improvements.

> Ladies, we act like a perfect wife more than we actually are one.

Now don't misunderstand me; Ms. Perfection really wants to be a good wife. She has all the right tools for it, and she has the willpower and desire to succeed. But in her quest for perfection, she has worked herself into a bad mood even before her husband comes home at the end of the day. And by that time, she does not have to try to impersonate a woman with a grudge on her shoulder about having to be so perfect—she truly is one! And her husband is out of luck.

THE PERFECT MOM SYNDROME

This portion of the chapter could be an entire book. I would write one if I thought it would actually sell! But perfect mom syndrome won't allow a well-meaning mom to buy something with a title like that in a public place like a bookstore.

After all, if someone saw her buying that book, it would totally blow her cover. The truth is that moms impersonating perfection can't bear the thought of owning up to the reality that there is, in fact, no such thing.

God didn't waste any time breaking me in on this one. My introduction to motherhood came in the tiny form of Graham Scott Whittle, our firstborn son. He came as expected, forty weeks on the dot, to two very inexperienced parents with a lot to learn. And from that point forward, nothing—and I do mean nothing—was as expected.

Graham was a difficult baby. He cried often and loud. He did not sleep well. He disliked most food. And when he occasionally smiled, most of the time it was because he had gas. Those were rough, tough days.

At the time of Graham's birth, several of my close girlfriends were due to give birth to their first children also. There were five of us to be exact, and we were all novices at this motherhood thing together. One by one, we each had our children with the largest span between them being six weeks. As soon as we could get ourselves acclimated enough to get out of the house, we got together. We had coffee together, brunch together, and Bible study together on a regular basis. All of us and our blessed creations from God. It should have been a beautiful experience. If only we could have heard each other talk over all the crying, which was, incidentally, most of the time coming from my son.

As my friends would gather in a circle with their babies dressed in gender-appropriate hues of pink and blue, you could find me hunched in a corner somewhere, trying to attach my plastic nipple shield onto my lactating breast. Nursing my son was always my first response though it was usually a disaster. He would cry, and I would cry, and all I really wanted to do was go home and be alone with my baby and our tears. I couldn't understand why my friends had the happiest, most well-mannered babies I had ever seen. My baby was nothing like theirs, and it hurt me to admit it.

In my frazzled new mom state of mind, I didn't realize that my behavior was hardly the cause of my son's outbursts. He was, after all, only a few weeks old! But I wanted to have the perfect baby so much that I was convinced my son was rebelling due to my lack of mothering skills. A month or two later, we found out our vocally blessed child had a severe case of acid reflux. Though Graham has grown into a very loving, responsible young man, I can still remember the feelings of inadequacy I had those first few agonizing weeks of being a mother.

I got over the perfect mom syndrome really fast. And thank goodness I did because since that time, I have watched friends and acquaintances struggle with it in a major way. The setting may be the playground, swim class, church nursery, or a family get-together, but the conversation is generally the same. "I don't know why he's acting that way! He never acts like this! I think it's because the house was too hot last night and he didn't sleep very well." Or "She really is a good baby. I can't believe she is crying like this . . . she never, ever cries. Even when I was cutting her nails and I accidentally snipped the end of her finger, she only gave a small whimper and then just got right up and started playing again. She must be sad about her grandma not getting to come for a visit."

Please. While I am sure it does make your baby sad that she won't get to see her grandma, and I'm sure he was not altogether comfortable in a stuffy house, any seasoned mom will tell you that there does not have to be a good reason for a child suddenly turning selfish, whiny, or even (yes, I'm gonna say it) downright bratty. Human nature has taken care of that without the help of outside factors.

Sometimes the perfect mom syndrome causes us to fall into the comparison trap with other moms. We see other moms and their children at story time at the bookstore and, while we are eager to meet a potential playmate for our child, we are determined to retain our image as perfect mom with perfect offspring. We size up the competition to see what statistics we might need to rattle off to the other moms, in order for them to know that we will not be easily matched or readily dethroned. After all, we have been programmed to believe that behind every perfect child is a perfect mom. And we take that role very seriously.

Since going to the bookstore for story time, I have met three-month-olds who can crawl, eighteen-month-olds who can read, two-year-olds who can spell, and six-year-olds who can translate Hebrew—at least, all in their mothers' minds. I am constantly reminded in these settings of our ongoing need to prove to our peers that we are pictures of perfection. We want so much for our children, and our desires are good ones, for the most part. But it's hard to be a parent when we are trying to be a perfect mom all the time. So I say, the jig is up. Let's put an Out to Lunch sign in the window of the perfect mommy shop. It's break time.

> Sometimes the perfect mom syndrome causes us to fall into the comparison trap with other moms.

THE PERFECT PACKAGE

The *perfect package* is the woman who knows it all, sees it all, does it all, whips it up for dinner, and sells it for a profit. (You know, she's the one you and I are intimidated and annoyed by.) She dresses impeccably, has money to burn, and sews her own curtains. But she calls them *window treatments* since she knows the importance of semantics. She manages her household, stays in touch with her friends, organizes neighborhood get-togethers, and doesn't break a sweat. She returns phone calls promptly, decorates her home professionally, and never misses her boss's birthday. She is overworked yet never stressed. She has a Colgate smile and a size 4 body. She finds time to scrapbook, run marathons, and serve on the town council. She is the personification of a perfect package.

By the way, she may or may not be married. The perfect package is different from the perfect wife or perfect mom while they share many of the same characteristics. Seeking perfection in outward appearance is certainly one of them. The perfect package is focused on making her outside look better by any and every means necessary, which may include tweaking, nipping, tucking, pulling, stretching, bleaching, manicuring, lasering, zapping, and camouflaging. While there is nothing necessarily wrong with any of these things, there is a dangerous societal pressure that motivates the perfect package to seek these procedures. And there is definitely a problem with that!

But perfect packages don't stop there. Since they are constantly researching how to present perfection to others, they are fully aware of their need to be *evolved* on the inside. Their bookshelves are lined with self-help books. They TiVo pop psychologists and listen to lectures on "Ten Days to a Better You." The perfect package first needs to *feel* perfect in order for her to sell others on it. And it's become a full-time job.

> The *perfect package* is the woman who knows it all, sees it all, does it all, whips it up for dinner, and sells it for a profit.

Though we typically think of Ms. Perfection as one of our peers, being programmed to present oneself as a perfect package can start at a very early age. I recently got a heart-tugging e-mail from one such former perfect package. I have known Tiffany for many years, but I have not seen her since high school. Though I rode to school with her nearly every day, I had no idea of the personal pain she was experiencing. Here is her story, in her own words:

> I spent the first twenty-five years of my life trying to be perfect. I come from a strong Christian family with high expectations. I learned from a very young age that the more I pleased my parents, the better I felt about myself. That began to carry over into every relationship I had. If I pleased you by being perfect, pretty, happy, confident, and spiritual, then you would like me . . . thus, I would like myself. My self-worth depended on everyone else's approval of me.
>
> After a while, the load became too much to bear, and I developed an eating disorder. I kept up the act of being supergirl, the daughter everyone wanted, but then I would throw up in the church bathroom after Wednesday night supper. I would lead a small group at camp and talk about how God loves and accepts us, no matter what our flaws. But then I saw so many flaws in myself that I wouldn't eat

the whole week at camp. I would lead worship at a weekend retreat, and at night I would raid the food supply and then purge in the host's home. I thought I didn't deserve God's love, forgiveness, or grace because I wasn't perfect.

That is how I lived for so many years. My eating disorder ruined every relationship that I had, but all the while I was singing on the praise team and going on mission trips. I was even engaged to a seminary student. I faked it with the best of them. I believed the message of God's grace that I was sharing with others; I just didn't believe that I was good enough for it because I wasn't perfect.

Finally, I decided I was not even going to try to act perfect anymore. I was going to rebel. I called off the engagement, transferred colleges, joined a sorority, and lived it up! I didn't darken a church door, and I didn't care. I thought, *If I can't be perfect, then I will be everything I have been taught perfect isn't.* I drank and smoked and did many things that I now wish I could take back. Eventually, I wore myself out and faced the fact that I was miserable. I could hear God calling me to come back to Him, and I didn't have to be perfect before I did it.

It is only since then that I have been me. I am not perfect, and I don't try to be anymore. Trying to be perfect is so exhausting, and there is never an end to it. No, I am not happy all the time, superconfident, or the tiny size I once was, and I have lost the fake smile altogether. I have learned that peace comes from my relationship with Christ, not my weight, my clothing size, what car I drive, or how many church functions I attend. Peace does not come from pleasing others, but from obeying God. So now I strive for obedience—and I bring Him my flaws and all.

Fortunately, Tiffany discovered her charade of perfection before it was too late. Whether it is an eating disorder or another form of perfectionism that drives you to appear more together than you really are, Ms. Perfection takes on different forms and manifests herself in different ways.

Young or more mature, single or married, childless or a mother of multiples, Ms. Perfection is easily impersonated by women across the country. We want to be the perfect wife, perfect mother, and perfect woman all wrapped up in a perfect package. Even though we know in our hearts that it's not possible, we still strive for perfection. And just like Tiffany, it is killing our souls and hearts in the process.

three

MS. CONFIDENCE

*Such confidence as this is
ours through Christ before God.*

—2 CORINTHIANS 3:4

Hands down, it was the strangest meeting I have ever participated in.

One Thursday night in the summer, a ministry colleague
and I were scheduled to meet with a woman who offered a
service we were looking for. She came into the room with a
confidence I had rarely seen the likes of before. "Good evening,
ladies," she offered professionally. "Oh, hi there," I casually
said. My colleague and friend followed suit. "Good to see
you." The woman said nothing back to either of us but took
her seat and reached into her bag for a notebook.

She was dressed impeccably in a tailored suit and matching high heels. Although wearing nice dress pants and a crisply

ironed shirt, I was no match for her streamlined look. I wondered why I hadn't worn a jacket to our meeting. I could tell by my friend's expression that she was having the same kind of thoughts. The woman pulled her notebook out of her bag and looked up at us. "I have one hour. Only one. That is all. Let's get down to business, shall we?"

Even the most type A person in the world wouldn't have turned her down. I took my cue to begin and started right away, not wanting to waste her limited time. "Well, sure. Let me catch you up to speed on what has been going on, where we are at this point, and what we are looking for from you."

I had barely gotten the words out when she interjected, "Excuse me, please. I appreciate that you are trying to brief me, but I'm the one who called this meeting. So I would like to tell you what I am willing to do rather than what you need me to do."

Completely thrown off, I swallowed hard and tried my best to hide my surprise at her abruptness. Hiding things well is not exactly my specialty, but I knew I had to go into actress mode to survive this meeting! I sensed the woman's need to be in charge, and I obliged. Actually, to be completely truthful, I didn't have time to protest, since she gave no room for comment.

For the next fifty minutes, we had a very professional conversation, with feedback and pleasant banter. Opinions were shared and details were given, with the woman we were meeting with still very much in charge. Ever mindful of our one-hour limit, I was just about to suggest we wrap up our meeting when something completely unexpected happened. The woman stopped, dropped her pen on the desk, and looked my friend and me in the eyes. Her face had suddenly changed, and her eyes began to fill with tears. "I'm sorry if I sounded kind of harsh at first. I've had a really bad day. Honestly, ladies, I need prayer."

Her stern demeanor began to dissipate as she shared with us about her college-aged son and what he was going through. He had been struggling with depression, and she was clearly concerned about him. He had revealed to her that day some things that made her motherly heart heavy with concern.

My friend, who had been uncharacteristically quiet, spoke up. "I have a son who struggled with depression too. He really went through a terrible time a year ago, and I know exactly what you are going through." I listened, fascinated, as these two women began to openly share struggles and common concerns . . . two women who only marginally knew each other moments before. The professional distance of our demeanor had evaporated, and a spirit of sisterly love and care had emerged. We ended the night as a circle of three, clasping hands and praying for this woman and her family in their time of need. And a meeting that started out with a confident woman on a tight schedule ended with a vulnerable woman in tears with time being the last thing on her mind. Ms. Confidence had left the building, and she was definitely not coming back that night!

Scenarios like this take place every day in America in groups of women. It may be in a corporate setting, a church setting, a community setting, or even a playground setting, but it happens all the time. Ms. Confidence can be wearing a business suit, a jogging suit, or a bathing suit, but you will definitely know her when you see her. She will be the one who has no problem carrying on a conversation, running the show, or letting you know how confident she is. Believe me, in one way or another, she will make sure everyone knows that.

BIG, HONKING, CANDY-APPLE-RED FLAG

I have a girlfriend, Kate, who is often frustrated by a good friend of hers, Allison. Having been friends for several years, my usually self-assured girlfriend often feels put down when she is around Allison. Even though they have shared interests and a good rapport, Allison is a few years older than Kate and tends to mother her more than Kate would like. Allison offers advice about most everything, and she multitasks like the best juggler in the circus. When Kate has a need, all she has to do is call Allison, who will make all the appropriate concessions to help her get through it. On the surface, Allison seems like an ideal friend.

But though she is a very capable, helpful friend, Allison is not likely to share openly her heart with Kate. She won't be the one to call Kate for a favor, nor will she be the one to cry on anyone's shoulder. Kate, who is perhaps the most tender and loving person I have ever known, has talked with me about this on several occasions, and she always says the same thing: "I don't know, Lisa. It's like Allison thinks I'm lost without her and wants to be like my mother. But sometimes I'd like to know I was there for her . . . that we were more like friends, helping each other out. But one thing's for sure, she definitely doesn't *need* me. I don't really think she needs anyone, to tell you the truth."

When Kate tells me things like this, it sends off the biggest, brightest, "blinkingest" (okay, not a word, but you get the visual) red light in my mind. And to my very sincere and frustrated girlfriend I always reply, "That's just what Allison *wants* you to think."

Well, what do we expect a confident woman to do? Wear a big neon sign that says, I Need People? I doubt it. In fact, Ms. Confidence, and those under her tutelage, would not get caught dead wearing a sign like that for fear of blowing their confident cover. For them, as it is for so many of us, it is not acceptable to show that we need someone when we are trying so hard for people to see us as self-sufficient, strong, independent, and fearless. So we choose to portray a confident woman with it all together in order to save ourselves the pain that might come with people seeing our vulnerabilities.

> We choose to portray a confident woman with it all together in order to save ourselves the pain that might come with people seeing our vulnerabilities.

Often, women I become good friends with tell me they admire my confidence and strength. Because of my type A personality, I tend to choose friends who are a bit more laid back and emotional than I am. I am more of the warm while they are the fuzzy. I have tried to be fuzzier, but it just doesn't happen naturally for me. Things just work better for both of us when I am the strong one, and they are the soft ones.

If there is a crisis, my friends know to call me. I will be "on." After all, that is how God has gifted me and who He created me to be, and I function well in these types of situations. But you want to throw me for the biggest loop in the world? Ask me to switch roles with my friends and have me call *them* for advice. Now that would take an act of God.

In recent self-reflection, as a matter of fact, an act of God *did* occur in this regard. As often happens in married couples, it was a lesson taught to me through an interaction with my husband. Okay, let me get downright honest. The truth is it all came about as a result of a huge fight one night.

I really don't remember what triggered the fight, but I do remember that Scotty and I were sitting in the study, in our usual fighting stance of him in my personal space and me trying to retreat from the conversation. "Why are you so distant from me, Lisa?" he asked. "I don't know, okay? And I am too busy right now to talk about it," I answered. "Just leave me alone . . . please." Scotty pressed on with the conversation despite my protest. "Talk to me, Lisa. I don't feel close to you right now." His words were sincere, and I took notice. He was right, after all. For weeks, I had been extremely busy with conference planning, writing, speaking, and caring for the household to the neglect of my poor husband. And it wasn't just him feeling it—I didn't feel close to him either. But I didn't want to admit it. So I gave him the silent treatment instead.

Aggravated by my lack of conversation, Scotty began to try to engage me in an argument to get some sort of reaction out of me. "Man! Why are you so stubborn, Lisa? You don't care about me, do you?" I could see his face starting to redden, and his eyes were beginning to get watery. I desperately wanted to reach out to him and share my feelings. I wanted to, but I just wouldn't let myself. I sat there with a coldness that scared even me, and I remained silent. Then all at once, something inside of me broke. The dam that had been holding back my tears suddenly wasn't keeping them contained any longer.

"I am so sorry, honey," I said, sobbing. "I have been so strong for such a long time that I don't know how to be weak. I love you. And Scotty, I need you." A sense of calm came over me as I reached for my husband, and we held each other tight. He graciously forgave me for my attitude, and I forgave myself for the damage it had caused in our marriage. It was a beautiful ending to a difficult night. God had revealed to me that though I had great strength and could handle many things, I had a *vulnerability* problem. And by admitting that I *needed* my husband, I was actually allowing myself to be vulnerable and exposed before him, myself, and God. It was hard for me, but it was a powerful thing for me to do. Sadly, it had taken me only eleven years to do it.

> God has placed us on this earth with other people to be companions, friends, and brothers and sisters in Christ to walk with us through our journey.

The truth is we really *need* only God. If everything and everyone else was stripped away, it would be excruciatingly painful, but we could survive. But God has placed us on this earth with other people to be companions, friends, and brothers and sisters in Christ to walk with us through our journey. I mean, think back to the very creation of women. Adam didn't exactly need Eve. After all, he had God. But God, in all of His graciousness, wanted to provide Adam with someone who would be his helper and companion in life . . . someone who would make life fuller and richer and much more exciting and fun! So, in a very earthly sense, although Adam didn't *need* Eve to survive, he was meant to walk on this earth *with* her.

When we portray confidence to such an extreme degree as I did that night with my husband, it robs us of the joy that comes with exposing our souls to a trusted companion. Ms.

Confidence is often so afraid of rejection—either because of past hurts or past experiences—that she prefers to stay in her confident shell and not let the soft side of her emerge. But she soon begins to realize that it's very confined in there!

In her book *Strong Women, Soft Hearts,* counselor Paula Rinehart talks about this issue in her chapter on vulnerability. She says:

> The strength of vulnerability is a curious mixture of discovering your heart and sharing your real self, as best you can, with people God has put in your life. You can't shut down on the inside without quelling the very passion that makes the journey worthwhile. Those walls around the heart take buckets of energy to maintain and God has better things for his children to do. When we close off our hearts, we dishonor him.[1]

So while my friends may admire me for my strength and counsel, the truth is I admire them . . . women who are open and vulnerable and real and genuine and without pretense. Those are the things that truly take strength.

REALLY . . . *CONFIDENT?*

If Ms. Confidence has a fan club, actress Kirstie Alley should be elected the president. After all, anyone who can bare herself in front of millions of TV viewers on the *Oprah* show in a bikini (at the age of fifty-seven) is one secure woman! Brave? Maybe. Shameless? Possibly. Confident? Definitely.

Ms. Confidence herself would approve of Kirstie's confident display of her body. She is, after all, promoting empowerment and assertiveness and freedom of expression. She may or may not choose to get on national TV in a bathing suit, but she will gamely applaud someone who will! The idea of making one's own decisions about her body and what to do with it is an idea Ms. Confidence highly esteems.

Making decisions about your own body seems like the epitome of confidence. It has become a gender-empowering thing in our society to own our sexuality and form a kind of identity around doing what we want to do. After all, only a truly confident woman takes control of her body in such a way that allows her to share it openly with others, expose it freely, and use it to her advantage. Right?

> The idea of making one's own decisions about her body and what to do with it is an idea Ms. Confidence highly esteems.

I was recently at home, stuck in bed while sick with the flu. As I was flipping through the channels of my TV, I came across MTV, the cable channel known for its primarily teen audience. The program was unfamiliar to me, but it immediately caught my attention. An attractive girl in her early twenties (I'm guessing), clad in an itsy-bitsy-teeny-weeny bikini, was running through a high-powered sprinkler while an audience of mostly young men was laughing, cheering, and jeering as she became soaked by the water sprayer. Finally getting to the end of the water trail, the young woman stopped and took a moment to smile and relish in the attention of the cheering males. She flung her wet hair back like she was on a calendar shoot and stuck out her chest as if displaying a prized collection. She collected her towel and the eleven dollars she was paid to perform for the guys. It was a dating show, and although the guy wanted to date her, she decided she would take the money instead and enjoy both it and the national exposure (in both senses) that she got from her watery performance.

After seeing something like that, people might call that young woman confident. They might consider her to be in control of her own body and doing what she wanted to do with it. But watching her, I had to ask myself, have we, as women, really become so disillusioned with what society tells us is a confident woman that we would choose to perform fantasy scenes in near-nakedness for men in order to be cheered on as a sport? If this is confidence, please give me a pass.

> Sadly, in our society, the way many women view our sexuality seems to be the litmus test about how confident and strong we are.

Now, although you may not believe me, I am seriously all about girl power. No, I'm not a feminist, but I love the idea of women being empowered to do things and accomplish goals and live in an emotionally healthy and independent way. What separates me from feminist ideals is not the way we desire for women to be viewed by society but the way we plan for women to get there.

Sadly, in our society, the way many women view our sexuality seems to be the litmus test about how confident and strong we are. One of the aspects of popular feminism today is the idea that in order for women to be fully free, they must also be *sexually* free. As this reasoning goes, a truly strong woman is one who is free to explore her sexuality with consenting adults in any way she likes. After all, the feminists say, whatever we decide to do with our bodies is *our choice*, and we should not be hindered in any way in making these choices about our sexuality and everything else.

Considering what we have seen so far about confidence, I have to ask myself my original question: would a truly confident woman take control of her body in such a way that would allow her to share it openly with others, expose it freely, and use it to her advantage? Would a truly confident woman be so self-assured that she had no real emotional need for others? If not, then how does a truly confident woman exist in today's world?

TRUE CONFIDENCE

The bad news / good news for Ms. Confidence is quite significant: confidence is not something merely worn. That is (bad news), confidence can't be layered on with our clothes for the day, and (good news) it can't be taken off or removed by anyone else when it is truly present. The kind of confidence that is impersonated for certain occasions will soon become like Cinderella's sparkly coach that turns back into a pumpkin at midnight. It will fade away with the first sign of opposition from a colleague or in an insecure moment with a friend. Even if Ms. Confidence can hold on to a certain level of poise and self-assuredness for a period of time, eventually she will crash and burn into a heaping mess of tears, racked with feelings of self-doubt.

> The bad news / good news for Ms. Confidence is quite significant: confidence is not something merely worn.

If a woman's confidence is dependent on her looks, what happens when she gets older and things begin to go south and wrinkle? If a woman achieves confidence in her job, then where does it go if she gets demoted or passed over for a promotion she has worked hard to get? If a woman obtains her confidence through the successes of her children, then what happens when her child goes down a destructive path of drugs or alcohol or lands in jail? Where does a woman's confidence go when her husband leaves her for another woman? In a moment of emotional exposure, where does a confident woman go to hide her true feelings from others?

The reality is that no matter how confident we as women want people to think we are, there are moments for all of us when the layers are not quite thick enough to keep us completely insulated. We were not made to live in a completely self-reliant state, regardless of how empowering that sounds. After all, Jesus acknowledged our human weakness when He said, "I am the vine; you are the branches. If a man remains in me and I in him, he will bear much fruit; *apart from me you can do nothing*" (John 15:5; emphasis added). And the apostle Paul clarifies that God's plan "does not, therefore, depend on man's desire or effort, *but on God's mercy*" (Rom. 9:16; emphasis added).

> The reality is that no matter how confident we as women want people to think we are, there are moments for all of us when the layers are not quite thick enough to keep us completely insulated.

But wait. While the bad news may be hard to hear, the good news is almost too good to be true! And in a strange way, it makes the bad news seem nearly as good. Remember, the good news is that true confidence can't be taken off or removed by anyone else. It all comes down to who our confidence is in, where it lies, and why we have confidence to begin with.

Society's suggestions about how to be a confident woman often contradict the truth about where real confidence comes from. Consider this recent list from *Redbook* magazine, entitled "10 Habits of Confident Women":

1. Make a grand entrance.
2. Work the room.
3. Recover gracefully.
4. Tell a great story.
5. Stay calm.
6. Ask for a raise.
7. Be a good haggler.
8. Overcome fear.
9. Don't be intimidated.
10. Tell a joke.[2]

Hear the overwhelming theme running throughout this list? All of these ten habits are things that can be done or, in keeping with our clothing analogy, worn. None of them, however, come from within—as something that exudes out of us because of our secure belief in God. So if the folks at *Redbook* are correct, Ms. Confidence is successfully confident as long as she wears her confident clothing and performs to the best of her abilities. But what happens when she runs out of great stories to tell? What if she can't think of a good joke to drop that night?

> True confidence comes from only one source—an inside Source—and it cannot be bought, sold, put on, or manufactured.

No, confidence cannot come and go as easily as the world says it does. True confidence comes from only one source—an inside Source—and it cannot be bought, sold, put on, or manufactured.

I recently came across a poem by an unknown author entitled "A Strong Woman vs. a Woman of Strength" that says a lot about the difference between these outlooks:

A strong woman works out every day to keep her body in shape . . .
> *But a woman of strength kneels in prayer to keep her soul in shape.*

A strong woman isn't afraid of anything . . .
> *But a woman of strength shows courage in the midst of her fear.*

A strong woman won't let anyone get the best of her . . .
> *But a woman of strength gives the best of her to everyone.*

A strong woman makes mistakes and avoids the same in the future . . .
> *But a woman of strength realizes life's mistakes can also be God's blessings and capitalizes on them.*

A strong woman walks sure-footedly . . .
> *But a woman of strength knows God will catch her when she falls.*

A strong woman wears the look of confidence on her face . . .
> *But a woman of strength wears grace.*

A strong woman has faith that she is strong enough for the journey . . .
> *But a woman of strength has faith that it is in the journey that she will become strong.*

While most women desire to be strong and fearless and self-sufficient, we are disillusioned into thinking that what we *do* is what makes us confident and strong. It's in the realization of where true confidence comes from that we are truly able to be that woman. And, in turn, people sit up and take notice of our confidence and see that it can't be shaken with circumstances.

Jesus gives us the answers to every spiritual dilemma, and confidence is no different. After all, He created us and knows where we are weak and what we lack. Though women are by no means lesser in Jesus' eyes, we were not meant to simply mirror men in temperament, demeanor, and actions.

A NEW PERSPECTIVE ON CONFIDENCE

Make no mistake about it, both men and women struggle with having confidence. Let's look at the apostle Paul as an example. He certainly knew something about confidence. After all, he survived many hardships and trials, he had great influence among fellow believers, and he had been uniquely equipped by God with amazing visions and revelations. But Paul had a flaw that kept him from believing in his own self-sufficiency. He poignantly describes his situation in 2 Corinthians 12:6–10:

> If I had a mind to brag a little, I could probably do it without looking ridiculous, and I'd still be speaking plain truth all the way. But I'll spare you. I don't want anyone imagining me as anything other than the fool you'd encounter if you saw me on the street or heard me talk.
>
> Because of the extravagance of those revelations, and so I wouldn't get a big head, I was given the gift of a handicap to keep me in constant touch with my limitations. Satan's

angel did his best to get me down; what he in fact did was push me to my knees. No danger then of walking around high and mighty! At first I didn't think of it as a gift, and begged God to remove it. Three times I did that, and then he told me,

My grace is enough; it's all you need.

My strength comes into its own in your weakness.

Once I heard that, I was glad to let it happen. I quit focusing on the handicap and began appreciating the gift. It was a case of Christ's strength moving in on my weakness. Now I take limitations in stride, and with good cheer, these limitations that cut me down to size—abuse, accidents, opposition, bad breaks. I just let Christ take over! And so the weaker I get, the stronger I become. (MSG)

Though we don't know what Paul's handicap was, it clearly gave Paul a fresh perspective on confidence. Despite his many ministry successes (and failures too), Paul knew his confidence had to be in God for his ministry to be effective. God gave him physical limitations so that this otherwise-capable man would not trust in his own abilities. Paul knew that only His Lord could bring him the confidence he needed to persuade people to listen to him. If he tried to put confidence in his own abilities as Ms. Confidence would, he wouldn't have made it very far.

So what about us as women? How do we become fearless, empowered, and independently secure women, despite our own handicaps, natural tendencies, and very nature? Is it possible? Is it ever! It's all in redefining those buzzwords we hear about Ms. Confidence that we can get the hands-on application we need to be that girl! So let's consider a new set of definitions.

Fearless: A complete state of being for a woman who rests in the strength of her God. "The fruit of righteousness will be peace; the effect of righteousness will be quietness and confidence forever" (Isa. 32:17).

Strong: A resilience that goes beyond any tangible or physical condition and is unmatched in its fortitude. "For the LORD will be your confidence and will keep your foot from being snared" (Prov. 3:26).

Empowered: Comes from knowing who we are in Christ and who, by His strength, we can become. "[I am] confident of this very thing, that He who has begun a good work in you will complete it until the day of Jesus Christ" (Phil. 1:6 NKJV).

> God says that when we put our confidence in the right place (in Him), our lives will be blessed!

Independent: Recognition that our relationship with God is deeply personal and our need for anyone else but Him diminishes. "For you have been my hope, O Sovereign LORD, my confidence since my youth" (Ps. 71:5).

Emotionally Healthy: The desire to please only one source— that is, Jesus Christ; the opinion of anyone else pales in comparison to what He thinks of us. "So we are always confident, even though we know that as long as we live in these bodies we are not at home with the Lord" (2 Cor. 5:6 NLT).

Accomplished: What we do for God becomes the central and primary focus of our lives. What we accomplish on this earth can be gratifying but does not make us who we are.

"And now . . . continue in him, so that when he appears we may be confident" (1 John 2:28).

God says that when we put our confidence in the right place (in Him), our lives will be blessed (Jer. 17:7)! Our confidence comes from knowing not only whose we are but also who He is.

four

MS. HAPPINESS

*He will yet fill your mouth with laughter
and your lips with shouts of joy.*
—JOB 8:21

I heard a fable once about a beautiful maiden who lived in a little village where many young men wanted to marry her. Several men had asked for her hand in marriage, but she always refused them. They would promise her things if she would marry them . . . extravagant and wonderful things, but she always turned them down.

A frog in the village decided that he would try a different tactic to see if the maiden would, indeed, be intrigued enough to accept his marriage proposal. So one day, he said to her, "Fair lady, if you will marry me and kiss me, I will turn into a handsome prince. And you can come to live with me in my castle, where you will cook for me, clean for me, serve me, and cater to me for the rest of your life . . . and you will be very, very happy."

The beautiful young maiden had certainly never heard an offer like this before, so she gave it some thought. After considering the offer, she surprised everyone in the village by taking the frog home with her that night. The village was abuzz about the strange relationship between the maiden and the frog and amazed that she had finally said yes to a marriage proposal. The next morning, the people were even more surprised to find out the truth about what happened after the odd couple had gone home: the fair maiden had herself a great feast of frog legs for dinner that night!

> Happiness is not always what it seems, and someone can easily impersonate happiness without actually having it.

The fair maiden was no dummy. What sounded like an unbelievable offer from a well-intentioned amphibian was nothing more than a manipulative tactic to get something from an innocent girl. But she didn't take the offer and had a great meal, to boot. Smart girl. I guess she was in on the secret about true happiness . . . that happiness is not always what it seems, and someone can easily impersonate happiness without actually having it.

Curiously, in some way we believe that happiness can be bought, earned, or achieved. American poet Amy Lowell once said, "Happiness: We rarely feel it. I would buy it, beg it, steal it, pay in coins of dripping blood, for this one transcendent good."[1] We desire to be happy so much that we are willing to do most anything to gain it.

But have you ever stopped to consider that the feeling of

happiness can come and go depending on the circumstances? Case in point: consider hot fudge sundaes. I don't know about you, but hot fudge sundaes can make me really happy when I'm craving one. Especially with an extra shot of whipped cream on top. Ahhh, pure bliss. Happiness, really.

Or how about shopping? I have conferred with my girl-friends on this, and we agree that nothing makes us happier than seeing a great-looking jacket on clearance. Happiness, achieved.

A new haircut has been known, at times, to make me happy. (Though sometimes it makes me really, really sad!) Simple things like making it through a green light when I am in a hurry and not burning the dinner makes me really, really . . . extremely happy! So when I stop and think about it, I'm not 100 percent convinced that our standards for happiness are really all that high most of the time.

> A lot of things can make us feel happy for a time. But a lot of things can also let us down almost as quickly as they perked us up.

A lot of things can make us feel happy for a time. But a lot of things can also let us down almost as quickly as they perked us up. No, I don't think happiness is what we are really after. I think it's something else entirely.

But still, we try to find happiness. Oh, how we try. We are on the never-ending search to find happiness in life . . . so much so that we rival the Griswolds on their quest to find Walley World. Society has played a large part in our search, pitching to us the notion that the way to find true happiness can be found in yourself. Sounds easy enough. So we keep on trying.

WHERE'S THE SOURCE?

By nature, we tend to seek the source of things. For example, when we walk down a busy city street and a rotten stench pervades our sense of smell, we instinctively turn and look for the source. When we hear a fire truck in the distance, we look out the window to see where it is coming from or where it is going. During dinner, when an obnoxious patron behind us is talking a bit too loudly on his cell phone, we crane our neck to see just who is ruining our dining experience by his reverberating voice. Our natural tendency is to look for the source of things to satisfy our curiosity and to help us gain a better understanding of our current situation.

I remember one time being in church and hearing a clicking noise. I leaned over to my husband and whispered, "Do you hear that? It sounds like someone is clipping their nails! Surely not!" As the sound persisted, I became more and more determined to find the source of such an annoying sound. And in a worship center that seats nearly three thousand, that is quite a feat.

My eyes darted about during prayer time, the offertory, and announcements, until they finally rested on a girl in the front row with a cast on her arm. I strained to see her, looking down at her arm . . . and yes, clipping her nails. After all my searching, I had found the source of the methodical clicking sound in a sea of church people packed beside each other in the pews like sardines in a can. Thinking back now, I still can't believe that the girl was on the front row grooming herself in the middle of church . . . or that I located her in the midst of so many people! I had simply followed the sound of the noise to find the source.

I can think of another time when I went looking for the source of something. This time, my quest was driven by an even greater annoyance. Last winter we discovered that we had an infestation of mice, evidenced by the chewed holes in the bottom of the boxes in our pantry and the trail of droppings we found in and around our kitchen. I was horrified at the thought that the rodents were somewhere in my kitchen, eating the food intended to nourish my family! My husband and I determined to get rid of the mice, but we knew we needed to find out where they were coming from. If we got rid of them without finding their point of entry, we were likely going to continue to encounter more of the rodents in the future.

After several weeks of trap laying and mouse catching, we ended up with a grand total of seven mouse carcasses and two very frustrated homeowners. Though we caught an entire family of mice, we never found the source of their entryway, which greatly concerned us. And even now, when the weather gets cold, we still hold our breath, thinking that we will see a recurrence of our mouse problem. Since we didn't find the source, we can't be sure that the problem has been, so to speak . . . completely *eliminated.*

The same principle is true of Ms. Happiness. She is the outward personification of a jovial girl, even though she is still searching for its inward source. Though able to act happy, since she has never truly found the root of happiness, she is forced to continue looking for it in places it will likely never appear.

MS. HAPPINESS'S TACTICS

Unfortunately, Ms. Happiness's A-plus efforts just aren't enough to produce the results she desperately desires. And her humanistic quests are often the same ones we try in our search for a happy life. See if you recognize any of these.

You Can Make Yourself Happy

Society tells us that self-awareness will produce a happy and fulfilled life. But I wonder . . . if our own self-awareness can make us happy, then why aren't we happy? After all, in recent years society has urged us to concentrate on ourselves, so we have read books and attended conferences and joined support groups intent on increasing our self-awareness, yet we have found no real success in its results.

Robert E. Quinn, professor and business leadership authority, once said, "It is our hypocrisy and self-focus that drains us. When we become purpose centered, internally directed, others focused and externally open, we discover energy we didn't know we had."[2] Often, the more we invest in ourselves, the emptier we feel. Have you ever noticed that? It's a strange irony, but it's true. The more time you spend thinking about *you*, the less satisfied you are with yourself or anything else. If we look to ourselves to provide the happiness we need in life, we are barking up the wrong tree. Otherwise, we would have found it, bottled it, and sold it to every corner drugstore. No, happiness cannot be found inside of us, no matter how hard we try to make it be true.

> Unfortunately, Ms. Happiness's A-plus efforts just aren't enough to produce the results she desperately desires.

Years ago, a song by a Grammy-award-winning recording artist scored big on the charts. The lyrics encouraged us to let the children find love and significance inside themselves.

While I firmly believe that we are to love and embrace the persons God created us to be (and I enjoy great '80s music), I am troubled by the message of that song. Yes, it is healthy to be content with ourselves, and it is good that everything "is well with my soul," as the old hymn says.[3] As an advocate of good Christian counseling, I strongly believe in the value of mental health, but I don't believe it comes from the happiness achieved through simple human efforts.

> Happiness cannot be found inside of us, no matter how hard we try to make it be true.

Someone You Love Can Make You Happy

A similar message is being sent our way in society's claim that one can find happiness through a relationship with someone else. Yet to demonstrate the fallacy of this belief, we need to look no further than the men and women who have been involved in extramarital affairs.

A friend of mine recently went through a really rough year when her husband left her for another woman, who was his coworker and friend. She was devastated by the betrayal and left to pick up the pieces of a broken life with three young children. A strong believer, my friend was firm in her faith that God would see her through this massive life storm and get her to the place of restoration and peace. But at the time it happened, bitterness was her constant companion. And I could see why.

During one of my friend's discussions with her estranged husband about what happened to bring them to this place, she questioned why they could not work it out despite what had occured between them. He answered her with the words no married woman ever wants to hear: "You just don't meet my needs anymore. Being with her makes me really happy, and I want to be happy." Call me cynical, but I have a high level of certainty that the so-called happiness in this relationship will not last.

And this man is not alone in his thinking. Many people have gotten involved in emotional and sexual affairs at times when they were seeking happiness. According to some reports, more than 40 percent of married women cheat on their husbands. With such a high statistic, I wonder how many of those 40 percent would say that they did it because they were no longer happy with their spouse. I can only guess that the percentage would also be very high. The sad reality is that in our ultimate pursuit of happiness, women are also looking outside of their marriages.

> Seeking an outside source to make us happy will never do the trick in the long term.

I came across a poignant piece written by Crystal Boyd in her book *Midnight Muse*. Though I don't know her personally, in reading her words, I get the sense that she has experience in seeking happiness from an outside source.

We convince ourselves that life will be better after we get married, have a baby, then another. Then we're frustrated that the kids aren't old enough and we'll be more content when they are. After that, we're frustrated that we have teenagers to deal with. We'll certainly be happy when they're out of that stage.

We tell ourselves that our life will be complete when our spouse gets his or her act together, when we get a nicer car, are able to go on a nice vacation, when we retire. The truth is, there's no better time to be happy than right now. If not now, when?[4]

Seeking an outside source to make us happy will never do the trick in the long term. Yes, being a wife can make you happy. Being a mother can make you happy . . . in a very real and special way. Finding happiness from a relationship with another will make you happy until it doesn't. At which point, it will take another relationship, adrenaline rush, or emotional high to keep you there.

Something You Have or Do Can Make You Happy

I heard a story once about a farmer driving a pickup truck who encountered a despondent-looking man sitting by the side of an old country road. Troubled by the man's demeanor, the farmer pulled over, walked over to the man, and asked what was bothering him.

"There is nothing in life that makes me happy, sir," said the man. "I have plenty of money, so I don't have to work; therefore, I am on a personal journey to find something more exciting and entertaining than the life I have at home. So far, I haven't found it!"

Without speaking a word, the farmer snatched the man's backpack, threw it into his truck, jumped behind the wheel, and sped off down the road. He drove half a mile down the road and then eased his truck onto the side shoulder. There he waited for the man he had just robbed.

A few minutes later, the miserable man appeared, looking unhappier than ever because of his loss. When he saw the farmer in front of him, holding out his backpack to him, the man ran toward him, shouting with joy. "That's one way of producing happiness," the farmer said, smiling.

The farmer was fully aware of what he was doing when he took the unhappy man's backpack, and his actions illustrate the idea of happiness coming from something we have or something we do. The world's mantra insists that personal perfection can make you happy. *Spend more*, *indulge more*, and *have more* are seen as the golden tickets to happiness and contentment, and women are buying into them right and left. Yet for all our indulgences, we are still severely unhappy.

In many ways, our life pursuits compare closely to those of King Solomon, the third king of Israel and David's chosen heir. Like many of us, Solomon mistakenly believed that the pleasures of life could and would bring him ultimate happiness, and he tried many avenues to find it. His avenues included what I call the four Ws: wine, women, wealth, and wisdom. Though we may not relate to Solomon's vast wealth, we can certainly relate to his quest to find happiness through physical relationships, gaining more knowledge as a means to facilitate self-worth, and seeking fulfillment in the pleasures this world has to offer.

> The world's mantra insists that personal perfection can make you happy . . . Yet for all our indulgences, we are still severely unhappy.

Yet for all of those pursuits, late in Solomon's life, he looked back on the things that did not bring the happiness he craved. After personal reflection, Solomon writes, "I said to myself, 'Come on, let's try pleasure. Let's look for the "good things" in life' . . . In this way, I tried to experience the only happiness most people find during their brief life in this world" (Eccl. 2:1, 3 NLT).

Solomon gives nuggets of practical truth throughout the book of Ecclesiastes. Then, in a final beckoning for truth, he writes the last chapter with his concluding thoughts: "Don't let the excitement of youth cause you to forget your Creator. Honor him in your youth before you grow old and say, 'Life is not pleasant anymore' . . . Fear God and obey his commands, for this is everyone's duty" (12:1, 13 NLT). Written so long ago, it's as if Solomon's words were written just for us today, in our quest for happiness.

A VERY REAL PROBLEM

According to the National Institute of Mental Health, more than twenty million people in the United States suffer from depression.[5] The US Food and Drug Association reports that one out of five women in the US has depression.[6] The Mayo Clinic, a leading facility with expertise on health, states that twice as many women as men will experience depression.[7] But we don't need to hear the statistics, since we already know they are true. Many of us know all too well because we have personally experienced depression or know someone who has. Though often well concealed, depression is a very real problem in many seemingly happy homes across the country.

No one is immune to this problem, no matter how happy she may seem on the outside. Just ask comedian Chonda Pierce, an unlikely candidate for clinical depression. In her book *Laughing in the Dark*, Chonda writes openly about her struggle with depression after many years of performing stand-up comedy. Although Chonda made thousands of people happy with laughter, she was not able to pull herself out of a self-professed "dark" and "gray" world. Her journey through depression is an example of how even the most seemingly happy people can struggle with this very real and difficult issue.

Stories such as this often leave me to wonder if, like Ms. Happiness, we act happy on the outside to please others, silently leaving us to hurt on the inside? Do we mask the way we truly feel with medications and facades, hoping that no one will dip deeper to find out what's really going on with us? One thing is certain: many of us (like King Solomon) are allowing our addictions to money, sex, drugs, shopping, and eating to lead us down a path of discontent rather than happiness in our quest for an eternally exuberant life.

The ironies about what produces true happiness are all around us. A World Happiness Survey taken not long ago showed shocking results. Bangladesh, one of the poorest countries in the world, ranked as the happiest nation in the world! A country with so little that it lacks even some of what we would consider the necessities of life is *happy*! Ironically, the all-too-prosperous United States ranked quite low. In this same survey, the US placed forty-sixth on the happiness roster, putting us behind India (fifth-happiest place in the world) and others like Ghana and Latvia, Croatia and Estonia. Though we have an abundance of anything we desire, Americans are not fully satisfied; we long for more. In fact, this study showed that people in rich countries, including Austria, the Netherlands, Switzerland, Canada, and Japan, are significantly unhappier than their poorer counterparts in countries

> Could it be that like Ms. Happiness, we act happy on the outside to please others, silently leaving us to hurt on the inside?

such as the Dominican Republic and Armenia. Clearly, some element to happiness is missing.[8]

UNITED WE SEARCH!

Finding happiness just may be what unites all of us, regardless of our personal life situations. Anne Frank once said of happiness, "We all live with the objective of being happy; our lives are all different and yet the same."[9]

One thing is for sure, you can't tell a happy person by the smile she wears, despite what Ms. Happiness wants you to think.

Many of the happy faces we put on center around our jobs, whether at home or in the outside workplace. My girlfriend Kim recently told me about her experience with feigning happiness in the midst of a tough job situation:

When I first moved to Charlotte, I started a job selling office supplies from business to business. I stuck with this job for about thirteen months until I came to a breaking point. The last few months of my job were especially trying. I would wake up with dread of facing yet another twelve-hour day. On my way to work, I would mostly just cry and pray.

I showed up at the office and slapped on a fake smile. We had very upbeat meetings from cheering to high-fives, all of which came out of the will to simply make it through one more day. Part of my job consisted of interviewing potential employees, and I will never forget the conversations where I was trying to sell them on our company. I told them how great it was and the benefit of what I was doing.

One candidate asked me a very simple question one day: "Do you enjoy what you do?" I smiled and somehow managed to say, "Absolutely." I hoped she didn't hear my voice crack as I was fighting back tears.

On the days when I was driving around with my candidates, we would stop at a fast-food restaurant for lunch and I'd let them stand in line to order while I would go to the bathroom, lock myself in a stall, and call my husband. At times all I could get out was, "This is a tough day; please pray for me." I would let my emotions release, clean my face, and within minutes head back out to the table, sit down, smile, and begin presenting to them our business structure. I got really skilled at pretending I was happy, when on the inside, I was truly miserable.

My sweet friend Kim, like so many others, portrayed the happy little worker going to work in order to keep the truth about how she really felt about her job from becoming known. Like Ms. Happiness, Kim had learned the art of pretending.

> One thing is for sure, you can't tell a happy person by the smile she wears, despite what Ms. Happiness wants you to think.

Many of us, like Kim, long for a happy life and are searching for a purposeful and positive existence. The truth is that if happiness could be characterized by a smile, we would all be living in the land of happy, eating at Grins Bar and Grill and shopping at Smiles "R" Us. Instead, we have become expert smilers and shiny, happy people. And although we have at times tried to pack up and move, for some reason, we are still taking up residence in Sadtown, USA.

HAPPY, HAPPY? . . . JOY, JOY!

I am guessing that you could probably use some good news right about now. Don't worry . . . despite the truth I've shared about my doubts of finding happiness by yourself, there *is* cause to celebrate. I have saved the best part of this chapter for last—and yes, it's really that good.

Respected author C. S. Lewis once said, "We are half-hearted creatures, fooling about with drink and sex and ambition, when infinite joy is offered to us, like an ignorant child who wants to go on making mud pies in the slum because he cannot imagine what is meant by the offer of a holiday at the sea."[10] I don't know about you, but the idea of a holiday at the sea makes me want to go there now! With the beach being one of my favorite vacation spots on earth, this idea is quite enticing to me. But what about you? Still not convinced about where to find what you seek? Still wanting to "make your own mud pies" in a do-it-yourself effort toward happiness? Then please allow me to give you one last illustration, if you will, to convince you of what source to seek.

> I prefer to go straight to the Expert when it comes to the subject of true happiness.

My husband and I went to Disney World on our honeymoon. We loved the idea of fun and excitement in the most magical of places, and we had a great time there together. While we were there, we visited Epcot Center, and it soon became my favorite place at Disney. We decided to eat at a French restaurant on the premises, and we made our reservations. Right away, a waiter came to our table and greeted us: *Bonjour!*

After taking our drink order and getting some recommendations for dishes, the waiter left our table to get our drinks. I commented to my husband about how impressed I was with the waiter's accent and knowledge of the country's foods and how surprised I was at how well he played the part of a Frenchman. My husband informed me that all the servers at the various countries' restaurants in Epcot Center were required to be of that nationality in order to better represent that country and to make the experience for the customer more authentic. I could see why that was important; I had begun to feel as though I had been magically transported to France and was no longer in the United States! It was a great time for us that night because we were in the hands of an expert when it came to French food.

Like my experience at Epcot Center, I prefer to go straight to the Expert when it comes to the subject of true happiness. Just as Disney knows the value of using authentic sources for the best results, so we need to recognize the authentic Source for our best results for a fulfilling life. And the first step in finding it just may be in changing one simple word.

If you search a Bible concordance for the word *happiness*, you will soon find out what I did: the Bible doesn't have much to say about happiness, but it has lots to say about *joy*. Could it be that the formula for happiness has been under our noses all along, all due to the fact we are using the wrong word? Here are a few verses on the subject, from the Expert Himself . . .

✦ You have made known to me the path of life; you will fill me with joy in your presence, with eternal pleasures at your right hand. (Ps. 16:11)

✤ The precepts of the LORD are right, giving joy to the heart. The commands of the LORD are radiant, giving light to the eyes. (Ps. 19:8)

✤ You turned my wailing into dancing; you removed my sackcloth and clothed me with joy. (Ps. 30:11)

✤ The LORD has done great things for us, and we are filled with joy. (Ps. 126:3)

✤ Though you have not seen him, you love him; and even though you do not see him now, you believe in him and are filled with an inexpressible and glorious joy. (1 Pet. 1:8)

Get the picture? Happiness is not the holy grail. Real joy is where it's really at. True joy comes from within when we are operating in our life in the way that pleases God. And that's not by faking people out with our facade of happiness but, rather, being filled up with joy by the power of the Holy Spirit.

I love the old song we used to sing in church called "I've Got the Joy." Its tried message is simple yet true:

I've got the joy, joy, joy, joy down in my heart. Where?
Down in my heart. Where?
Down in my heart.
I've got the joy, joy, joy, joy down in my heart. Where?
Down in my heart to stay.

The song continues on, letting us in on the results of such heart-filled joy:

And I'm so happy . . . so very happy.
I have the love of Jesus in my heart, down in my heart.

And I'm so happy . . . so very happy.
I have the love of Jesus in my heart.[11]

The true and lasting source of our happiness comes from the joy that fills our hearts and overflows into the paths of those around us. When we go to the real Source of joy, we find the answers we need to secure our contentment in life forever.

> True joy comes from within when we are operating in our life in the way that pleases God.

This joy cannot be revoked, and it won't be changed according to our circumstances. And with this thought in mind, we have cause to celebrate! Because while happiness cannot readily be achieved and is often impersonated, the reality is *joy* that comes from our heavenly Father is easily achieved and readily offered.

Psst. Pass that on to Ms. Happiness. She's on her way to Smiles "R" Us.

five

MS. SPIRITUALITY

To be spiritually minded is life and peace.
—ROMANS 8:6 NKJV

Her name is not even mentioned in the Bible. As a matter of fact, we know very little about the woman whose story is told in Luke 8 as well as in the gospel of Mark. We do know one thing: she would not have been voted Ms. Spirituality by her peers in a spirituality contest. I doubt she would have considered entering in the first place. She was not the type to have been the chairperson of the finance committee at church. She likely would not have been in the choir, and she probably wouldn't have attended a weekend women's retreat. She was far too much of an outcast for any of that. Ostracized and scrutinized, she wore a cloak of shame and sin, rather than a bright metallic button that says: I Am Superspiritual. She really didn't need the button, since people already knew she wasn't . . . at least, that's what they thought they knew.

She is a bit of a medical mystery to us Bible readers since her physical diagnosis is not fully disclosed in Scripture. Whatever it was, it was pretty severe as it caused her to bleed continuously. Her body ravaged by the disorder, the emotional damage that came from the ostracizing of her peers wreaked equal havoc on her soul. When she enters the scene in Luke, she has come to see Jesus, hoping upon hope that He will heal her from her plight.

Luke 8:42–48 recounts the story:

> As Jesus was on his way, the crowds almost crushed him. And a woman was there who had been subject to bleeding for twelve years, but no one could heal her. She came up behind him and touched the edge of his cloak, and immediately her bleeding stopped.
>
> "Who touched me?" Jesus asked.
>
> When they all denied it, Peter said, "Master, the people are crowding and pressing against you."
>
> But Jesus said, "Someone touched me; I know that power has gone out from me."
>
> Then the woman, seeing that she could not go unnoticed, came trembling and fell at his feet. In the presence of all the people, she told why she had touched him and how she had been instantly healed. Then he said to her, "Daughter, your faith has healed you. Go in peace."

Can you just imagine the scene? I can only guess at what the highly spiritual people in the crowd that day thought of this woman, so clearly in need of a touch from God. She was totally going against type when she reached out to Jesus . . . only a person worthy of His touch would or should seek Him in most people's eyes. Yet Jesus attaches a highly spiritual word to her—*faith*. I am amused by the thought of the button-wearing spiritualists in that scene doing a double take when they heard Jesus commend the sinful woman's faith. After all, most of them probably thought such words would be reserved for them!

Were she to exist in that day, Ms. Spirituality would certainly desire to relate to the button wearers, *not* to the unclean bleeding woman behind the thick cloak. Her self-importance would surely be diminished if she were to in some way identify with the sickly woman, and more importantly, her standing in the Christian community could be compromised. And that is just not a risk Ms. Spirituality is willing to take.

> I am amused by the thought of the button-wearing spiritualists in that scene doing a double take when they heard Jesus commend the sinful woman's faith.

Ms. Spirituality, after all, has the same goal in mind as do all the other role-playing characters who have gone before her in this book. But for Ms. Spirituality, the stakes are a bit higher. Her status in the church and in her community depends on how well she performs when the camera is rolling. She is determined to show people just how spiritual she is, and she knows exactly how to go about doing just that.

MS. SPIRITUALITY'S SPIRITUAL CHECKLIST

If Ms. Spirituality had a checklist, I imagine it would look something like this . . .

☑ Attends church *and* Sunday school (or small group), rarely missing a week.

☑ Volunteers for nonprofits and Christian organizations every chance she gets.

☑ Knows proper "Christianese" and uses it frequently.

☑ Collects money from others for the less fortunate.

☑ Listens to Christian music and Christian radio and watches only Christian TV.

☑ Often wears a Christian pin or T-shirt and has a Christian bumper sticker or emblem on her car.

☑ Attends at least one women's conference per year.

☑ Prays for missionaries faithfully.

Though these things have some merit and are important to her, when Ms. Spirituality really needs to impress, she pulls out all the stops . . .

❖ Attends midweek church activities and leads at least one church ministry.

❖ Starts up a Christian organization.

❖ Journals, blogs, and writes her own devotionals.

❖ Gives away her own money to the less fortunate.

❖ Has no cable or XM radio . . . and if she's really spiritual, she has no TV!

❖ Has a personalized Christian license plate.

❖ Attends more than two women's conferences a year, or coordinates at least one.

❖ Goes on overseas mission trips every year.

Of course, those are in no particular order of importance since Ms. Spirituality doesn't pick and choose but, rather, does all of them. And most of the time, she does all these things well. After all, being spiritual is a full-time job for Ms. Spirituality. She works hard at it, and she takes her job very seriously.

Now don't get me wrong, some of the things Ms. Spirituality does are worthy causes and are certainly pleasing to God. The point is not that Ms. Spirituality *does* these things, rather, *why* she does these things. Remember, it's all in the performance, not in the act itself. It's a role that is played when it is deemed necessary to impress someone, yet it holds no real depth whatsoever. It's like the person who swims in the shallow end of the pool bragging about what an accomplished swimmer she is, never getting near the deep end for fear that her lack of skills will be found out!

As I reflect on that list, I find myself seeing the value in most all of these spiritually labeled things. After all, I have either participated in or have felt convicted to participate in virtually all of them, and I truly believe that most of them have great worth in the eyes of God. The question is not if they are good things to do, but rather, are they things that

> The point is not that Ms. Spirituality *does* these things, rather, *why* she does these things.

make us more "spiritual"? Ms. Spirituality certainly thinks so. But are they? I guess that all hinges on what your definition of *spirituality* is.

I have come to realize in my research that it depends on whom you ask. According to ReligiousTolerance.org, "[Spirituality] is defined quite differently by monotheists, polytheists, humanists, followers of new age, Native Americans, etc. A common meaning is 'devotion to metaphysical matters, as opposed to worldly things.'"[1] In essence, spirituality is a state of being from one's own personal belief system and experiences. It is broad in its scope, and its definition will likely greatly depend upon whom you ask.

This definition blows Ms. Spirituality's theory right out the window, since she believes spirituality is based on performance, rather than a state of being.

SO WHAT'S THE PROBLEM?

Ms. Spirituality seems like a desirable woman to be. After all, aren't we *supposed* to strive to be spiritual? Shouldn't we reach for heavenly heights in our everyday life? Well, yes . . . and no. (If you are surprised by the no part, please keep reading.)

The yes part of that answer is rather simple. James 1:22 reminds us that some spiritual muscle is required in our relationship with God: "Do not merely listen to the word . . . Do what it says." The action verb *do* is included in that passage for a reason because in a very real way, our actions show that we are, indeed, followers of Christ! Remember the apostle Paul's description of the fruit of the Spirit? "But the fruit of the Spirit is love, joy, peace, patience, kindness, goodness, faithfulness, gentleness and self-control. Against such things there is no law" (Gal. 5:22–23). In this passage, Paul lets us know that the root of our honorable behavior comes from the Spirit of God. He clarifies that despite our inborn personality, we are not relegated only to behaviors that come naturally to us. This complex, Christlike spiritual fruit is possible if we are filled up by

> The problem comes when our performance of these characteristics takes precedence over the actual condition of our hearts.

the Holy Spirit of God. And it is important to display this fruit.

The Bible is filled with examples of people who displayed such characteristics. Hannah had great patience as she waited on God to give her a child (1 Sam. 1–2). Abigail, the wife of a mean-spirited man named Nabal, exuded faithfulness and goodness despite the difficulties in her marriage (1 Sam. 25). Leah, who has been called the most unloved woman in the Bible because of the rejection she suffered by both her husband and her father, exhibited self-control by staying focused on God in the midst of her inner turmoil (Gen. 29). Jesus' own mother, Mary, showed great love when she willingly accepted God's glorious mission for her to carry Jesus as her son . . . and then modeled an enormous amount of peace when He was brutally crucified (Luke 1–2; Acts 1).

> All of our good deeds and actions depend completely on the motive of our hearts.

These beautiful characteristics were displayed by godly women—ones we would all do well to emulate. There's no question about that. The problem comes when our performance of these characteristics takes precedence over the actual condition of our hearts. Remember the religious leaders in Israel in Jesus' day, the Pharisees and the Sadducees? It is interesting to note that although the people they led considered them to be spiritual, many times Jesus rebuked these leaders and made an example out of them as to how *not* to act.

In one memorable instance chronicled in Matthew, Jesus pointedly burst the Pharisees' spiritual bubble when He called them out as the hypocrites they were. Though they claimed Jesus and His disciples were breaking the Law by not performing the ceremonial hand washing before a meal,

Jesus took the opportunity to teach about the inner purity of the heart. Clearly disgusted by the Pharisees' pious attitude, Jesus quoted to them a stern rebuke from the prophet Isaiah: "These people honor me with their lips, but their hearts are far from me. Their worship is a farce, for they teach man-made ideas as commands from God" (Matt. 15:8–9 NLT). Jesus got the point across to the onlookers by calling out their supposed religious leaders in front of them!

All of our good deeds and actions depend completely on the motive of our hearts. If we strive to be spiritual just for the sake of striving, then we are wading in dangerous waters. The prophet Isaiah concurs with this truth, saying, "Your works are utterly worthless" (41:24). Ephesians 2:9 says our salvation is not based on our performance: "not by works, so that no one can boast." Romans 11:6 adds to this truth: "And if by grace, then it is no longer by works; if it were, grace would no longer be grace."

Bringing these verses into application for Ms. Spirituality, we must remember that the goal of Ms. Spirituality is how her spiritual self looks to others, not how it may actually be. Sadly, the church often plays a role in this, veering off the path God intended for us. I love the way Casting Crowns identifies this spiritual *dance* in this brilliantly written song, "Stained Glass Masquerade":

> *Is there anyone that fails?*
> *Is there anyone that falls?*
> *Am I the only one in church today feelin' so small?*
>
> *Cause when I take a look around*
> *Everybody seems so strong*

I know they'll soon discover
That I don't belong

So I tuck it all away, like everything's okay
If I make them all believe it, maybe I'll believe it too
So with a painted grin, I play the part again
So everyone will see me the way that I see them

Are we happy plastic people
Under shiny plastic steeples
With walls around our weakness
And smiles to hide our pain
But if the invitation's open
To every heart that has been broken
Maybe then we close the curtain
On our stained glass masquerade[2]

The writer of this song has our spiritual number, so to speak. Its sentiment is echoed in the minds and hearts of faithful churchgoers everywhere. The truth of this song is the same truth of this chapter: there are many people sitting in church pews, attending visitation, teaching a Sunday school class, and volunteering for a mission project who are actually lacking spiritual depth in their relationship with Christ. When people are all dressed up on Sunday morning, none of us can see what is really going on inside their souls.

FAUX SPIRITUALITY

There's no actual definition for *faux spirituality* in the dictionary. I've looked it up, and it's not there. But it should be. I have seen it firsthand, and I know it's real. How do I know it exists? I am the adult daughter of a pastor. Talk about a great platform to play superspiritual Christian.

I have always cherished and respected my upbringing in the church. My parents taught me an early love for my Christian heritage that to this day remains solid. I can honestly say that through all the trials I watched my parents endure in their ministry, I have never questioned whether the church institution is ordained by God. I can't say that about all the *people* in the church because we are all human and flawed. But the church, as a body, is precious and truly God's beloved.

So with that background, allow me to say this: in the church there are a lot of people who are playing the role of superspiritual Christian who could possibly not even be one. Sounds harsh, I know, but the truth is that you can't tell the soul of a person by the shell she wears. If it were the case, the impersonation business would be bankrupt, and there would be no reason for this book.

No, impersonations are rampant in the church. Ironically, church is the one place we should feel the safest from judgment by our peers, yet it's the very place we often experience the most rejection and legalism. Sadly, in many churches, grace is not always on the agenda. It's not that we don't want to be real . . . we just want people to see us as the perfect Christians we purport to be, even though the woman sharing the pew with us longs just as much as we do to share a real moment with a genuine person.

Just a few weeks ago, I saw this truth come into play with a simple yet meaningful interaction on a Sunday morning at church. My husband and I teach a thriving group of our peers every Sunday morning. We have grown to love each and every one in our class, and we are constantly welcoming new people to our group. Our motto has always been that we are "Real people . . . with real relationships . . . and a very real God." It is something we deeply believe, and we want to influence others while letting them know that we are far from perfect ourselves.

On this particular Sunday, a woman who had not previously visited our class came to see what we were all about. Though neither my husband nor I met her before class, she came up to Scotty afterward. With a large group such as ours, we are certainly aware of the hurts represented each week, but Scotty was nonetheless a bit surprised by what this visitor said.

"I wanted to come and check out your class. But I am nervous about bringing my husband since he doesn't typically like to come to groups like this," the woman admitted. "I wasn't sure what he would think about it because he is an alcoholic. But I was really excited when I started talking to the man sitting beside me about it, and he shared with me that he's an alcoholic too! Now I feel like someone here may be able to relate to him, after all."

Clearly, my husband and I do not desire to hear about someone struggling with an alcohol problem or an addiction of any sort. This example is in no way meant to glorify an addiction. But it is meant to show how the power of an honest Christian, struggling as he or she may be in life, can break down some of the emotional walls people construct out of fear of rejection by sharing their own personal truth. We can't always wear our hearts on our sleeves, and it's not always appropriate to share our personal struggles in public situations, but it is also refreshing to hear from a sincere person who desires to be real . . . sometimes at the expense of being perceived by others as spiritual.

But still we pretend. It's just less complicated, really. Impersonating a superspiritual person fluent in Christianese stops the intimacy of a face-to-face conversation with someone. But it can prevent other things too. It can stifle tears that need to flow, hands that need to be raised, prayers that need to be prayed, and decisions that need to be made. We trade reputation for repentance, and it costs us a lot. It costs us an intimacy that is sweet, both with our heavenly Father and our earthly family of God—and a real chance to be discipled by the spiritual authorities placed over us in the church. It is a hard habit to break and can be a humbling experience.

Several years ago, a group of college women asked me to speak at one of their monthly meetings. I was honored to be asked. I consider myself fairly far removed from my college experience, yet I still struggle with seeing myself as someone's mentor.

> We trade reputation for repentance, and it costs us a lot.

With about a month to prepare, I readied my talk. It was one I had done before, but I made some major revisions. I cut and pasted several messages together to make one, shaved it down to fit the time slot, and reworked the title. I was ready to share with these young women a message I felt was appropriate for them and meaningful for me.

The night came that I would speak, and I skimmed over my notes as I got ready. I drove to the location and went inside to meet the girls. They eagerly greeted me, and I was excited to spend time with them. As I moved around the room, I was flattered by their compliments and admiration. I was the picture of where they wanted to be in ten to fifteen years: with a loving husband and children and with promising ministry opportunities. I paused to meet each girl and find out something about her life. I knew this was the cream of the college crop, since they had forgone their weekend plans of dates and dinners to take time to hear from God. They were hungry for God's Word, and I was just the one to bring it to them that night.

I felt confident in the presentation I was about to give. After a brief introduction, I started in on the prepared talk. It was, appropriately, about female leadership.

As I took them through the reasons they might be unwilling to lead in something, I came to the all-important point of fear. I began to share examples from the Bible of people who could have had valid reasons to fear leadership, yet they stepped out and led, regardless. I could see the students' hearts being stirred as I shared familiar biblical names that meant much to them since they already knew their stories of faith. It was about that time that my perfect presentation went south.

I continued to rattle off biblical examples when I looked up and locked eyes with a girl on the front row. She was considered the leader of the group, and she was very grounded in the Word and in her faith. It was at that moment that she began to shake her head from side to side at an increasing rate of speed. First, it was a small motion, only detectable by me and possibly the girl sitting behind her. But that small motion soon became an overt headshake to rival windshield wipers on their highest setting. Clearly, I had said something she did not like or agree with, and she was trying to tell me so. I stumbled for a moment and then continued, making a mental note to check my notes later.

With all the professionalism I could muster, I finished my

talk. The usual buildup to the ending was not very climactic as I was still being distracted by the nonverbal communication coming from the front row. We said our good-byes, and I rushed out to my car, eager to get back to my own home. I did not ask the girl on the front row what I had said that she hadn't agreed with, and she did not ask me to stay for coffee. Something was definitely wrong.

I arrived home to a quiet house. The children were tucked in their beds, and my husband was asleep on the couch with the ball game still on the TV. Quietly, I entered my bedroom and turned on the light. I flipped off my shoes and reached for my slippers. Holding my notes for the message I had given, I began to flip through the pages to find the place that met opposition. When I read the bottom paragraph of page four in my notes, the color drained from my face.

I sat there, horrified, as I read and reread the words I had typed. I couldn't believe what I had done. In all of my cutting and pasting to create the perfect talk, I had inadvertently coupled a name to a fact that didn't match up. Sure, it was a P name. It was just the wrong P name. The fact I had mentioned was true for a Bible character whose name started with P—just not the P whom I had mentioned. The right P hadn't made the cut. Or should I say the paste.

Here I was, Little Miss Speaker with so much to share, yet I had shared the wrong information with a group of Bible students. My mentorship was a bust, and the bad part about it was I didn't realize why until it was too late. I'm ashamed to admit that I was too embarrassed to go back and make it right. It was simply too humiliating an experience for me to have been so focused on making a perfect presentation that I had forgotten to pay attention to what I was saying. I was worried about my image, and there was no room for damage control at that point.

While it is still embarrassing for me to share with you now, it is also hugely important that I do. I would be impersonating something I'm not if I wasn't candid about how completely flawed and imperfect I am! Fortunately for all of us, spiritual perfection is not a requirement to faith in Jesus Christ. Were it so, I would have long ago been disqualified. In this very humbling experience, I learned that like a car with a calibrated speedometer, there is a limit to how fast and far I can go. As human beings with human flesh, we are all that way. No matter how gifted or qualified we may be, we are bound to our human limitations and inadequacies. In truth, the more accomplished a person is, the more risky it gets to do anything without Christ. And that was a great lesson for me to have learned so early on in my speaking ministry.

> Fortunately for all of us, spiritual perfection is not a requirement to faith in Jesus Christ.

Though we seek it, our lack of spiritual perfection may be the best thing in the world for us since it reminds us that we are absolutely nothing without Christ. I love what Ravi Zacharias says about our faith in his book *Recapture the Wonder*:

> It is not about a ritual; it is about a relationship. It is not about the posture of the body; it is about the need of the soul. It is not about the times of the day; it is about the timelessness of His presence. It is not about appeasing God; it is about resting in His provision. It is not about culture; it is about truth. It is not about earning peace; it is the wonder-working power of God.[3]

A COMPLETELY DIFFERENT QUESTION

My good friend Monty once told me about a reputable leader in our government who approached him with a question. As the president of a national nonprofit ministry, Monty's spiritual reputation began getting around. The government leader had noticed, and he was eager to find out what Monty was all about. So he asked Monty an interesting question one day over lunch: "I've been watching you and wondering, are you religious?" Monty smiled and asked, "Religious about what?" The government leader's expression indicated to Monty that he was puzzled by this response. So Monty continued: "I mean . . . I am *religious* about watching Monday night football. I don't miss a Sunday at church or tee time at the golf course. I *religiously* brush my teeth every night before bed. So I'm not sure what you mean by that question." The government leader clarified, "What I mean is, are you a Jesus person?" Monty replied gamely, "Now that, my friend, is a completely different question."

> Perhaps in her quest for spiritual perfection, like many of us, Ms. Spirituality is asking the wrong question.

Perhaps in her quest for spiritual perfection, like many of us, Ms. Spirituality is asking the wrong question. She is looking at the ritualistic side of her faith, rather than the tangible expression of a deeply rooted love for God. Spiritual performance may indeed be a result of one's spiritual depth, whereby religion may not have anything to do with it. Were it so, it would be like planting tulips in your flower bed only to have daisies pop up: pretty to look at but not what you originally had in mind.

God's original plan was not for us to prove to Him that we love Him by performing to the best of our spiritual abilities. Rather, He is seeking today what He has always been interested in getting from us: a relationship with Him that is pure of heart and motive, the only goal in mind being to honor Him by doing His will.

- ✤ He won't ever mess us up or lead us astray. "For he guards the course of the just and protects the way of his faithful ones" (Prov. 2:8).
- ✤ He will never ask of us anything that will harm us. "The LORD will keep you from all harm—he will watch over your life" (Ps. 121:7).
- ✤ He offers to us the most amazing benefits if we follow Him, the likes of which have never before been offered and cannot be matched. "Praise the LORD, O my soul, and forget not all his benefits" (Ps. 103:2).

Putting it that way, which would you choose? To be religious? Or to be a Jesus person?

In Erwin McManus's book *Soul Cravings*, he outlines what he sees as the problem in our spiritual terminology:

Ironically, one of the very things that should draw people to God has actually repelled them from Christianity. Over the last two thousand years, the Christian religion has abdicated its unique view of the individual and has fallen in line with every other world religion. It's easier to run a religion if you can standardize everything, including the people. Religion, after all, has become one of history's most powerful tools for controlling people.[4]

McManus goes on to summarize what he sees as the danger in this *standardized testing* of religion as it relates to God: "Somehow we've equated conformity with holiness. Spirituality is more identified with tradition and ritual than it is with a future and a hope . . . The tragedy, of course, is that this has nothing to do with Jesus."[5]

So in a boxing match between God and religion, who would win? Think you know? Who would win a bout between God and spirituality? Hmmm . . . now that one may be a bit harder to call. Simply Google the word *spiritual* and you will come up with 88.5 million results. Think with me for a minute about a few of the things that some consider spiritual. To some . . .

> Karma is spiritual.
> Buddhism is spiritual.
> Ethical culture is spiritual.
> Humanism is spiritual.
> New Age is spiritual.
> Paganism is spiritual.
> Yoga is spiritual.

I don't know about you, but I'm not altogether sure I want to identify with any of these *spiritual* things. And what amazes me is the length people go to seek out the spiritual. In my research on this subject, I came across several offers for Free Spirit Coaching. Apparently some people are so desperate to find spirituality that they are willing to be "coached" by someone to aid them in finding it! Our need for spiritual answers in this life could not be more glaringly apparent.

THE TRUE LITMUS TEST

With all of the spirituality talk floating around out there, you may be somewhat confused. More questions than answers may be coming up, and it all may seem a bit contradictory. What identifies someone as a spiritual person? Should Ms. Spirituality continue spinning her heels to strive to prove that she, indeed, embodies what is spiritual? Is there any merit to being spiritual? Let me clarify this by drawing you to the amazing story of Moses. Within his story is a litmus test with which we can judge our spirituality in the way it really counts.

> True spirituality is about the awesome power of God showing up in a person's life to the point that people around her notice a difference.

You may remember that Moses was the strong leader of the Israelites. We read in Exodus that the Lord told Moses on more than one occasion to lead the Israelite people to the Promised Land. But like so many of us, Moses was apprehensive (if not scared) to do what God asked. Though he trusted God, his flesh continued to pull him back to unbelief.

After struggling with God about it, Moses finally came to the place of ultimate surrender. He figured out that running from God's will for him was completely futile, and his desire to please God superseded his fears and anxieties about his leadership role. It's true that Moses relented but not before presenting to God what his Lord already knew was on his mind:

> Moses said to the LORD, "You have been telling me, 'Take these people up to the Promised Land.' But you haven't told

me whom you will send with me. You have told me, 'I know you by name, and I look favorably on you.' If it is true that you look favorably on me, let me know your ways so I may understand you more fully and continue to enjoy your favor. And remember that this nation is your very own people." (Ex. 33:12–13 NLT)

Moses trusted God, but because of his insecurity in his own abilities, he was in need of reassurance from Him. Like a wise counselor, the Lord knew exactly what Moses needed to hear. He assuaged Moses' anxieties when He answered him, spelling it out for His servant in terms Moses would likely understand and appreciate:

I will personally go with you, Moses, and I will give you rest—everything will be fine for you. (v. 14 NLT)

Nearly convinced, Moses implored the Lord one more time, laying out his feelings and concerns in raw form. The complete confidence he had in God's supernatural power over his human capabilities is apparent:

Then Moses said, "If you don't personally go with us, don't make us leave this place. How will anyone know that you look favorably on me—on me and on your people—if you don't go with us? For your presence among us sets your people and me apart from all other people on the earth." (vv. 15–16 NLT)

The question Moses asked God in verse 16 could not make any clearer the distinction between someone who says she is

spiritual but lacks God-given depth and the person who actually *is* spiritual as it comes from the Holy Spirit and is in the
presence of Almighty God, with evidence of Him in her life.
This kind of spirituality goes way beyond good deeds and honorable actions. It is about much, much more than the number
of women's conferences attended per year. True spirituality is
about the awesome power of God showing up in a person's life
to the point that people around her notice a difference.

And when that happens, you won't even have to wear a
button to prove it's true.

part two

THE MASSIVE
COVER-UP

six

COSMETICS FOR THE SOUL

The law of the LORD is perfect, reviving the soul.
—PSALM 19:7

In 1994, I was a graduate student in Texas, struggling to pay my rent on a shoestring salary. Already working two jobs to make ends meet, I determined that I needed another supplemental income. As a proofreader to one of the school's vice presidents, I enjoyed the convenience of working on campus and the challenge of rising to a new level of professionalism by the example of a very learned man. Working in a counseling center for several hours a week kept me operating within my field and satisfied my need to help people better themselves and their lives. So when it came time for me to secure my third job, I knew just what I was looking for to balance out my work life: I wanted to find something that paid me a little to have a lot of *fun*. It was the only missing element in my work, and I wanted to find it.

My friend Martie asked me about my interest in working in the cosmetics industry, and I jumped at the idea. I had always looked at the salespeople behind the cosmetics counters and wished I were as beautiful and put together as they appeared to be. And besides that, I loved to experiment with makeup. After being hired by a well-established company and undergoing some training, I was on my way. It didn't take me long to learn the tricks of the trade, the artistry of applying makeup, and how to close a sale. I thoroughly enjoyed my job and always looked forward to my time at the counter.

I saw many different types of customers while working in cosmetics; a Saturday shift at the mall was a fascinating experiment in people watching. I have since forgotten many of the faces I saw while working at the makeup counter in Texas. But one customer, I can assure you, I will never, ever forget.

She approached the counter like many others, rather timid and lacking confidence as I had seen in other women before. But she was noticeably different, right from the start. Wearing a hat pulled down on her forehead and thick, dark sunglasses, she paused for a minute and then finally spoke. "Good morning," she said. "Can you help me?" She removed her glasses, and although a grown woman, the look in her eyes was that of a schoolgirl waiting for her punishment from a stern principal.

I paused before I answered, taking in the sight before me. I was glad she couldn't read my thoughts. *Whoa. Those are some pretty bad scars. I hope she doesn't want me to try to cover them up. Yikes! Do we even make a product that will cover up burns? What happened to her? I feel so sorry for her.* I wasn't altogether sure I could help her, but I welcomed her to the counter anyway. "Well, ma'am. I'm not sure, but let's give it a shot!" The woman looked genuinely relieved that we had gotten past the introduction and clearly now felt a bit safer with me.

"I need something to cover these up," she continued, pointing to the scars I had already noticed. I took a deep breath, said a silent prayer, and began to try to recall my training in makeup application though I am convinced that all the training in the world would not have been particularly helpful at the moment.

> How many of us are trying to conceal our feelings to cover up our broken souls?

The badly scarred woman and I worked together to see what result we could get with what we had. For the next thirty minutes, we experimented with colors and textures and consistencies of makeup. Determined to help her and her willing to let me, we dabbled in different application techniques and tricks of concealment. It took nearly an hour before we were satisfied with the result even though it was not a perfect solution to her problem. She left that day feeling a little better about what she saw when she looked in the mirror. But what our meeting triggered in me has lasted many years.

I came to realize that the jobs I held were more similar than I had originally thought. No, these women weren't coming to me for counseling, but many of them came to the counter looking to change something they didn't like about themselves. They sought this change with makeup and cosmetics on the outside while the patients the psychologist I worked for sought to salvage their internal souls. But all of them were trying to conceal things about themselves in order to hide the truth and escape rejection from others.

This story brings me to an important question to consider in this great charade in life we play. How many of us are trying to conceal our feelings to cover up our broken souls? We do this so others will see on the outside what we want them to see. We think we can fool people with our cover-ups, and maybe we can. But God wants us to be *real* . . . real to others, real to ourselves, and real with Him.

THE ORIGINAL COVER-UP CONSPIRACY

It starts in the very beginning of the Bible. No matter your church background, you are likely familiar with the story of Adam and Eve. These real-life characters in Genesis have been portrayed through the years in oil paintings, sculptures, and statues. In the images I've seen of them, Adam usually looks quite masculine, sparsely clothed, and more than a little bewildered while Eve usually looks seductive and womanly, and is almost always accompanied by a snake, representing the serpent (Satan) who tempted her and was the catalyst for the first big cover-up.

In case you haven't heard the story, let me briefly summarize it for you. After the creation of the heavens and the earth (Gen. 1–2:6), God created man and named him Adam (Gen. 2:7). He gave Adam a garden to tend to and get food from, with the exception of one tree (vv. 8–17). Because of His goodness, God did not want Adam to be alone, so He created for him a companion in the form of a woman, naming her Eve (vv. 21–22; 3:20). The serpent then lured Eve to sin by tempting her to eat the fruit from the forbidden tree (Gen.

3:1–5). Being manipulated by Satan's tricks, Eve ate the forbidden fruit and offered it to Adam, who also ate it (v. 6). Suddenly aware of their nakedness, they became uncharacteristically embarrassed by being seen by the other in their birthday suits (v. 7). But what Adam and Eve do after that is what interests me even more than the other amazing elements of this story.

> We use concealer—cosmetics for our souls—that will camouflage those places in our hearts that are uglier than we want to see.

Genesis 3:7 says Adam and Eve "sewed fig leaves together and made coverings for themselves." It's interesting to note that the very first thing Adam and Eve did when they sinned against God was to cover themselves with leaves, feeling exposed by their own sin. As a result, the first big cover-up after the world came into existence was what Adam and Eve did in the garden that day. And we have been trying to cover up ourselves, in one way or another, ever since.

We might not try the fig leaf approach, but in moments of exposure we often scramble to find an alternate personality, a better song and dance, or a more favorable angle to cover up what we don't want others to see. We use concealer—cosmetics for our souls—that will camouflage those places in our hearts that are uglier than we want to see. And the fact of the matter is that the source of Adam and Eve's sin and subsequent cover-up is the same source that chides us into believing that we are in dire need of a cover-up conspiracy of our own: the sneaky serpent himself . . . Satan.

IDENTITY THEFT

Somewhere in America today, at least one of us is losing our identity. But it's not in the way you might think. It's not by a computer hacker or a common con artist. It's not by misplacing our credit cards or giving out our social security number. Instead of a monetary loss, we are losing something much more significant. We are losing our identities in the form of our souls.

Let's face it: for most of us women, the prospect of losing anything is not our first choice. Even the most organized women lose things we wish we could find and desperately want back! On a daily basis, we are losing something . . . from a back to an earring, to our keys, to our best friend's favorite recipe for lasagna. We fear a lost wallet or a lost dog, yet we seldom even think about a loss that is happening to us right under our very noses.

It is a gradual occurrence for many of us. It sneaks up on us like our mother-in-law's birthday, and by the time we realize it, we are a day late and a dollar short . . . full of regret and excuses. We play the protective mother hen to our brood at home and even do our part as responsible citizens to try to protect the lives of others, yet we seldom protect the very thing that should be treasured by us above all else . . . our hearts and souls. How did such modern, godly women allow this to happen to us?

We Have Been Influenced by Society

We are the Dr. Phil generation. Like it or not, we are virtual junkies when it comes to collecting the knowledge the world has to offer in the form of self-help books, motivational seminars, and TV psychologists. We look to CNN and Fox News to tell us what we need to be concerned about and how our lives are going. We are glued to reality TV in the hopes that it will show us what real life is all about. Opinion polls and statistics guide our thoughts and beliefs, almost subconsciously. Society has a hold on us, and it doesn't plan on letting go anytime soon.

We Have Been Lied to by Satan

The master manipulator has done it again. And again. And again. Satan has been lying to us for a long time, but we seem to be buying into his lies now, more than ever before. *You are too damaged. You are unworthy of love. You have missed it. You'll never have a future.* The backyard bully has gone from subtle whispers to outright yells in our ears as he tries to convince us of our complete hopelessness in life . . . and we believe him.

We Have Been Hurt by Our Choices

Free will is a beautiful gift God graciously gave us when He created us. But our fleshly, flawed selves have made some bad choices along the way—and in so doing we have inflicted upon ourselves unnecessary pain that has caused us to lose a part of our very hearts and souls. We bought what society sold us: *if it feels good, do it.* It felt good at the time, so we did it. And now it doesn't feel good at all. We have tried and failed at controlling our own destinies, only to learn in the process that with free will comes the responsibility to own the consequences of the path we choose.

In Romans 12:9, the apostle Paul urges us to "cling to what is good." With the voice of worldly counsel speaking louder now than ever before, it is imperative that we are totally grounded in the Word of God and the truth of His message. It's the only way we can combat the influences of modern society about marriage, parenting, politics, and even our relationship with God. We must know who we are—who we really are—so that Satan's lies cannot infiltrate our thinking and permeate our lives. We need to let go of the guilt and regrets from the past that color our opinion of our future while acknowledging mistakes we made along the way.

> It is imperative that we are totally grounded in the Word of God and the truth of His message.

It is the *truth* that truly sets us free . . . not the truth according to Oprah or Bill O'Reilly or anyone else, but the truth according to God's Word and our heavenly Father. In a world that is spinning out of control, full of people losing their identities, the truth of God is not the most popular message, but it is by far the most important.

THE SHORT END OF THE STICK

I cannot tell you how many times my husband has ordered an exercise machine, a bottle of miracle weight-loss pills, or a muscle-building gadget only to be disappointed. Suffice it to say that the numbers of ordering versus the times actually enjoying aren't entirely equal. Bless his heart, like so many of us women, Scotty just wants to lose a little weight. (Though I don't think he needs to.) He gets excited by a new product and thinks that it will be the magic cure for his problem, only to face the reality that the problem is something internal, unable to be completely fixed by an outside source. And he winds up dissatisfied every time he tries something new to fix it.

Likewise, many of us are dissatisfied with the way life has turned out. Our disappointment has caused us to become increasingly displeased with our current situation, and therefore we feel as if we've gotten the short end of the stick in life. Everyone else's journey seems smoother, more exciting, and enviably fulfilling. Yet even the most accomplished people of this world struggle with the desire to have a more fulfilling life, oftentimes turning them into massive overachievers.

Jennifer White was one such overachiever who wanted more. This accomplished author and life coach wrote about her own struggles with seeking satisfaction in her life:

> I've lived my life completely dissatisfied no matter what I accomplished. It was never good enough, and I had to keep running to yet another achievement in search of satisfaction or fulfillment or whatever I thought I wanted. Funny, but no matter how much I accomplished, it still wasn't enough. I was featured in *USA Today* and *The Washington Post*. It was not enough. I built a thriving business with oodles of opportunities and great profits. It was not enough. Every day, I lived in a constant state of frustration.[1]

She continues as she poses a question to the reader:

> How many days do you walk around completely dissatisfied with what you have? You set a big goal, put the plan in place and go for it. But as soon as you reach the goal, you immediately say, "What's next?" . . . I know some of you believe this perpetual dissatisfaction is how you're supposed to live. Never-ending improvement, quality initiatives and striving to be perfect is what you base your success on. It's what

drives you, what makes you tick. And you think you're supposed to be dissatisfied to keep pushing yourself to live to your full potential.[2]

This popular writer, who reached many of her personal goals as a journalist and business executive, was dissatisfied with her life even though by society's standards she was a huge success. Her own feelings of drawing the short straw were likely hidden from everyone who watched her achievements. But the feelings were there; they were just really well hidden. Sadly, Jennifer White died suddenly only a few months after writing those words—a poignant reminder to all of us that life is short, and God wants us to be fully satisfied in Him while we are here.

> God's desire is for us to be real and open and honest and deeply and fully satisfied with our lives.

In the forty-ninth chapter of the book of Jeremiah, the prophet takes the message of God's just wrath to the wicked nation of Edom. The Edomites, descendants of Esau (Jacob's twin brother), were a prideful and sinful bunch, and God wasn't having it anymore. He sent Jeremiah, a somewhat reluctant messenger, to spread the word that He was going to destroy Edom, so they'd better watch out! In His message to the people, God assures the Edomites that no one can hide themselves from Him, by saying about Esau, "I will uncover his hiding places, so that he cannot conceal himself" (v. 10). God wanted to let the Edomites know in advance what He was going to do and that there was no need trying to fake Him out or seek out a cover. He was going to expose them for who they really were!

God is always merciful and just, even when He gets royally ticked off sometimes with the way we act. His desire is for us to be real and open and honest and deeply and fully satisfied with our lives. Need proof? Consider these verses:

✤ Praise the LORD . . . who satisfies your desires with good things so that your youth is renewed like the eagle's. (Ps. 103:1, 5)
✤ Satisfy us in the morning with your unfailing love, that we may sing for joy and be glad all our days. (Ps. 90:14)
✤ You open your hand and satisfy the desires of every living thing. (Ps. 145:16)

Satisfaction by the world's standards is not easy to come by. Just consider Anna Nicole Smith, the blonde beauty who died tragically in 2007. Born Vicky Lynn Hogan, Anna was in the prime of her life at age thirty-nine when her years of substance abuse, hard partying, and lavish lifestyle culminated in her death in a Florida hotel room. Anna had all of life's luxuries at her fingertips, and then some. She stood to inherit millions of dollars from her deceased older spouse. She was a celebrity of sorts, with all the fame she had ever wanted or craved.

But Anna was not a person who was truly satisfied. Her abandonment by her father and difficult relationships with her mother and other family members seemed to always follow her on her road to success. Her beloved son, Daniel, died tragically just ten months before Anna died, and by all accounts, Anna never recovered from her loss.

In the book of Isaiah, the Lord asks, "Why spend money on what is not bread, and your labor on what does not satisfy?" (55:2). Although Anna had the world and then some, she clearly couldn't deny her longing for someone to care for her, love her, and want to take nothing from her. Anna might not have known it, but what she was longing for was God. As far as I know, she died without discovering the true peace and real satisfaction that comes from a relationship with God. Although wealth and fame separated most of us from her, she was just like everyone else when it came to the longings of her soul. The psalmist expressed this longing as a desperate thirst: "O God . . . my soul thirsts for you . . . in a dry and weary land where there is no water" (Ps. 63:1).

In contrast to Anna's story, when we discover what we are really looking for, we find ultimate and complete satisfaction. Psalm 63:5 says, "My soul will be satisfied as with the richest of foods; with singing lips my mouth will praise you." Imagine eating a delicious meal at a fine restaurant and how satisfied you feel when you have eaten to fullness what was presented to you. That is how it is when we feed from the table of our Lord as He offers rich portions of Himself to us. We're fat cats when we feed off of Him!

In order to find full and lasting satisfaction, we have to look to the heavenly things, not the temporal things of this world. Our ultimate goal has to be to seek Him and His righteousness, above all else. That way, when we face our Lord, as all of us one day will, we will be able to say, "And I—in righteousness I will see your face; when I awake, I will be satisfied with seeing your likeness" (Ps. 17:15).

seven

THE FEELINGS WE CONCEAL

*He searches the sources of the rivers
and brings hidden things to light.*

—JOB 28:11

Have you ever looked at something and wondered what was behind that which was visible to you?

Ron Hutchcraft, author and communicator, once wrote about his friends' home. He details their great room, a room full of nice furniture and exquisite décor. He says that on a wall near the fireplace hangs a beautiful painting. Though it's a lovely addition to the room, Ron says that it has not always been there. His friends hung it there in order to hide a large, ugly hole when the wall behind the painting cracked. Since they are friends of Ron's, they shared this piece of information with him. Otherwise, he writes, he would have never known the hole existed since the beautiful painting was so thoroughly concealing it.[1]

Beautiful paintings often conceal our ugly places too. As women, we spend much of our lives trying to conceal things we don't want others to know about us. Sometimes it's as simple as trying to cover up our flabby thighs by wearing Spanx under our skirts. We use mints to hide our bad breath before we have a conversation with someone we don't want to blow away with our halitosis.

But we do the cover-up thing in other, much more important ways as well. We conceal our past. We keep our real agendas hidden. We mask our true feelings and cover up our sins. We just can't bear the thought of someone knowing what is really going on inside our souls, so perfectly hidden by the "beautiful" things they see.

So now that you've had a few minutes to think about it, I'll ask the question again. *Have you ever looked at something and wondered what was beneath that which was visible to you?*

Sure you have. Think about this food scenario for a minute. (Forgive me—I am a woman who likes her food.) You are at a women's get-together where everyone is supposed to bring a dessert. A woman

> As women, we spend much of our lives trying to conceal things we don't want others to know about us.

walks in with a dark, nonstick pan with a clear lid. You peek through the plastic and see a dreamy, whipped-cream topping, and you wonder what masterpiece of a dessert is underneath that yummy-looking surface!

Ask any mother of a young child, and she will tell you that given the option, a child will choose a plain brown paper sack sealed tightly with mystery toys hidden inside rather than a toy on the shelf in front of her simply because it is human nature to want something that is currently concealed from sight. We all desire to know what we are getting, whether it is in a dessert or a toy or a person.

Yet we usually do our best to conceal the truth from others. Why? Because of our feelings, we try to conceal these things from others in order to hide what is painful to admit even to ourselves.

INSECURITY

I nearly lost a friendship once over a game of Scattergories. It sounds silly, I know. But it's the honest truth.

We were visiting one of our best couple friends for the weekend. They live in another state—about 350 miles away—so to see each other at least once a year, we take turns making the trip. It was our turn to visit, and we had taken the kids out of school for a long weekend. The activities started soon after our arrival with our days and nights filled with museums, sightseeing, and great food and fun. Everyone was really enjoying themselves, and before we knew it, the weekend was nearly over.

The night before we were scheduled to leave, we decided to spend some quality couple time together, without the children. We ate dinner, cleared the dishes, and put the children to bed so we could get in a few board games to cap off the night. We sat down to a round of coffee and a game of Scattergories. The night was still young, and we couldn't have been having a better time.

There was a good-natured and easy banter between us

that traditionally accompanied our game playing. All of us are somewhat competitive by nature, and all of us are veteran board game players. In addition, on this particular night, all of us were also tired. We had enjoyed a jam-packed weekend filled with activities. Even though we all really wanted to play games, we also needed to get some sleep. But we chose fun over rest, and we started playing into the night.

We were almost ready to fold up the game and call it quits when a slight tremor began to occur at the game table. We were each playing a good game, and things were heating up between us. After my girlfriend's next turn proved successful, her husband began disputing the legitimacy of the move his wife had just made. As they were both stating their cases, their voices were beginning to rise, and my friend's husband decided they needed a third party to enter the scene to give a ruling on the call. With my husband in the bathroom, I was elected to the task of deciding who would reign victorious on this controversial turn. I sarcastically thanked my male friend for "throwing me under the bus" with him as I considered what I should do. I knew he was the one who was correct, but I also knew that if I sided with him, she would consider me a traitor to the girl power we had going on in the room that night.

"Uh . . . I don't know . . . I can see both of your points of view." I at first tried to slip out of my role through diplomacy. But they weren't having it. They pressed me for an answer, and I knew I would have to eventually give one. So I took a deep breath and reluctantly revealed whom I was siding with . . . my girlfriend's husband.

While it was hard on me to vote against my girlfriend, it would have been even harder for me to pull off an answer I didn't believe was correct. I was just being honest, and I hoped she would understand and take it well.

She didn't. It became abundantly clear to me by the look she shot me that she was not admiring my integrity or appreciating my honesty. To make matters worse, upon hearing my ruling in his favor, her husband started jumping up and down like a madman on a pogo stick, saying over and over, "Oh, yeah! Oh, yeah! Oh, yeah!" Things were going downhill at an alarming rate. My girlfriend began to shout two-word phrases at her husband I had rarely heard her say before, like, "Shut up!" . . . "Sit down!" . . . "Quit bragging!" and "You stink!"

Oblivious to her mounting frustration, he egged her on. "Oh, honey, it's okay. Everyone knows you are really smart. It's just not your night," he patronized as his wife started manically clearing the table, signaling to all of us that the game was now over. I had the right to remain silent, and I was exercising that right—which, incidentally, was not helping things either.

Irritated and now ticked off, my friend asked me why I had disagreed with her. I nervously saw the tide turning from her husband to me and my lack of good judgment in giving the final call. I calmly defended myself, outlining the reasons I did not feel her answer was right, at which point she starting listing the reasons I was totally wrong. Then, all of a sudden, this argument that had nothing to do with us in the first place took on the intensity of a matchup between a woman with her firstborn on the line versus a woman with her salvation at stake! We found ourselves battling back and forth, verbally, like a couple of women fighting over the last size-10 little black dress on the sale rack at Nordstrom. At which point, the confrontation turned ugly. And not forty-five minutes after it started, we ended the game and the night with my girlfriend insulting my cooking and my questioning her intelligence. So much for lighthearted game playing with good friends!

I am happy to report that our friendship with our fellow game players is still fully intact. With this incident a few years behind us, we can actually laugh at that ridiculous scene. But at the time, I was sincerely concerned that it might cost us our friendship. I sulked the entire way home and spent months afterward analyzing how it all went south. After all, I realized that as petty as it was, things like these have been known to break up female friendships! (Guys, on the other hand, usually end up in a conversation about sports five minutes after such an incident.)

As I reflected back, I came to the conclusion that the argument had nothing at all to do with who could claim bragging rights over a night of Scattergories. It was really all about one thing and one thing only: the insecurities of two women who happened to be playing a game together. The insecurities were already there; they were just brought out by a competitive board game between friends. We were both insecure about being seen as smart and sharp and capable in front of one another. Truthfully, I think we were less convinced of that about ourselves.

> All of us have had moments of insecurity, some lasting longer than others and of varying degrees.

I would venture to guess that as you are reading along, you can probably relate to my story in one way or another. All of us have had moments of insecurity, some lasting longer than others and of varying degrees. Women are notoriously insecure over our bodies, our abilities, our mothering, our relationships with our husbands, our reputations in the church, and our standings in the community. It is really no small wonder as to why we try to cover up our insecurities . . . it's much easier to emote frustration and anger than admit we are feeling slightly less than confident about ourselves!

Insecurity, by its simple definition, is a lack of self-confidence and an uncertainty in oneself. It's a self-esteem issue, really. But it's not a simple problem, and it can be a tool Satan uses to cause us to believe things about ourselves that result in less-than-genuine behavior toward others. It causes us to feel as though we are not as good as the next girl . . . not as pretty as our best friend . . . and not as capable as our coworkers. We feel insecure about something pertaining to ourselves, usually our looks or our abilities. It seems harmless at first, like it is hurting only us and no one else. But insecurity is not harmless at all. It can be a dangerous spark that can ignite into a flame and fuel something much more harmful: jealousy.

JEALOUSY

"Am I still in high school?" my friend on the other end of the phone asked me sincerely after having a run-in with a friend. "It all seems so juvenile; I honestly feel like I used to feel back when I would fight with a girl in algebra class over a guy we both liked! I didn't know that this kind of catty behavior could follow me into my adult friendships. I didn't realize grown women could act this way."

I could feel her pain. Not long before I, too, had a run-in with a woman I considered a close friend. It was not over who made the cheerleading squad or who wore better outfits . . . it was over much more hurtful matters, the matters of the heart.

It was an eye-opening experience for me to realize that a person I cared for and considered mature could act more like my high school nemesis than a treasured pal. And when I shared my experience with other women, they each had a story about a similar situation and difficulty with their girlfriends. The truth is, before I get too pious here, let me step up and say that I myself have been guilty of such petty and poor behavior. At some point, most of us have either been the recipients or the instigators of very hurtful behavior that threatens the kindred spirit we long to have with other females.

The reality is that adult female drama can be more dramatic than any teenage grudge or petty argument. It can be far more hurtful than the whispers behind our backs in the lunchroom at school, and it often holds much bigger ramifications. The stakes are higher now—much, much higher. In high school, we were jealous about guys, curfews, looks, who made homecoming court, clothes, and our parents' status. Today, as much older (and, supposedly, more mature) women, the jealousy is over cars, houses, children, marriages, jobs, looks . . . and our own status and standing in the community. We long for friendships with other women—we read books on it, and we search for it—but true friendships are often very difficult to find and much more difficult to actually keep.

I love what author and speaker Lisa Bevere says about this in her book *Fight Like a Girl: The Power of Being a Woman*. In chapter 2, entitled, "What If I Don't Like Women?" she writes:

There was a time when I was not particularly fond of [women]. Not only did I not like women, I resented being one. Therefore, I was not surprised by the concert of anti-female sentiment from my fellow sisters. I have heard one form or another of this sentiment expressed by women of all ages and walks of life.[2]

She further explains, a few pages later, that this aversion to female friendships isn't really about an ardent dislike for our own gender; rather, it's the dislike of how we often conduct and manage our friendships.

> It's not that you don't like women . . . you don't like the dance we are now doing. The costume is uncomfortable and the song is awkward. You have sought to distance yourself from shallowness, frailties, and failings, and this is not actually a bad thing. But it is not enough. Denying our gender will never move us from the problem dynamic to the answer.[3]

Most of the time, we do nothing to help debunk our own myth that females can't be friends. Many of us have determined to shy away from female friendships, resigning ourselves to the notion that it just isn't possible.

Though they were not female, we can certainly learn a lot from the relationship between famous friends in the Bible, Jonathan and David. Their friendship is recorded in 1 Samuel 18:1–4, where it says that "there was an immediate bond of love between them, and they became the best of friends" (v. 1 NLT). The commentary in my New Living Translation Bible further summarizes why their friendship worked so well:

1. They based their friendship on commitment to God, not just to each other;
2. They let nothing come between them, not even career or family problems;

3. They drew closer together when their friendship
   was tested;
4. They remained friends to the end.[4]

What a fantastic four-step process to follow! Just think of what would happen if we applied those principles to our own friendships with women.

On the other hand, look no further than the thirteenth chapter of Genesis to see how *not* to manage a relationship. Here we see the story of Abram and his nephew, Lot. Facing a potential land dispute, the situation between the two men got ugly. Instead of pulling together, they let petty jealousy drive them apart and parted company for good. Such pettiness is not relegated to just these two men in the Old Testament. Our own jealous dramas often cause us to sever female friendships.

Admittedly, I used to be a huge skeptic of the ability of females to have genuine female friendships. That is, until I met Colleen Cooney Lewis.

Now, don't get me wrong. I have had other precious female friends throughout the years. I still correspond with many of the girlfriends I made from a very young age, including Tina, the friend from the opening story in this book! And I do not want to slight them in any way or minimize their importance in my life. But even though I have had some wonderful friendships with females through the years, I still think I had somewhere hidden in my mind that

> The reality is that adult female drama can be more dramatic than any teenage grudge or petty argument.

females could never truly love each other the way I longed for in a girlfriend. Maybe it was because my family moved a lot, and I never got the opportunity to grow up with them. Maybe it was because my dad was a pastor, and I was always a bit insecure about the motives behind my friendships. Or maybe it was just . . . because. It really doesn't matter why, it just matters that I was once a nonbeliever in female friendships, and now I am a big believer in them.

My friendship with Colleen started in graduate school, when we were both in our twenties. We became fast friends, marrying just four months apart and serving as maid and matron of honor in each other's weddings. Since that time, our friendship has spanned job losses, marital conflicts, childbirth and child rearing, health concerns, mammograms, and surgeries. Twelve years later, we could not be closer. Colleen is like a spiritual sister to me.

After telling you all that, you might be surprised to hear me say that something is missing in my relationship with Colleen. But something is. There is a missing element in our friendship that makes our friendship work . . . we are simply not jealous of each other.

Colleen is skinnier and more outgoing than I am, and we both know it. I have some unique opportunities with my speaking and writing, and she has absolutely no desire to speak or write. She doesn't care how well decorated my house is, and I don't care if she is a better cook or party hostess than I am. She encourages me to entertain, and I consult with her on decorating ideas for her home. I give her makeup makeovers once a year, and she gives me new recipe ideas when I need them. But she provides me with so much more. Colleen allows me to share my deepest joys with her, and when I do, I never, ever detect an ounce of jealousy in it. And I never feel jealous of her successes or joys either.

I tell you this not simply to share about my best friend but also because I want to assure skeptics like me that a relationship with another female without pretense is truly possible. Though I never quite thought it to be true, my relationship with Colleen is living proof.

I often think of the friendship between Oprah Winfrey and her best friend, Gayle King, when I think of a successful friendship without jealousy. Both are accomplished women, and both are capable and strong and talented. They likely have things about the other that they admire and love, and they likely have different strengths. But I sense genuine love between them when Gayle appears on Oprah's show, and I suspect that it is because the missing element in their relationship is the same one that is missing in my relationship with Colleen: jealousy.

> There is a missing element in our friendship that makes our friendship work . . . we are simply not jealous of each other.

Female friendships are truly possible and really important. Females meet the needs of other females for conversation, support, and empathy, and they can greatly enhance one's life. But jealousy is the one thing that will stifle a female friendship before it even starts. It is a feeling we are not eager to admit we experience, even as we age, but it is an important reality to face in thinking about things we cover for.

LONELINESS

Remember Waldo? If you were around in the early 1990s, you probably do. Waldo was the cartoonish-looking character that became a pop-culture phenomenon of sorts. Books, video games, and toys were created when Waldo mania took the nation by storm, and many still exist today. The idea behind Waldo was to create a character who looked distinctive, was a bit nerdy, and could be picked out of a crowd of dozens of others in the picture with him. Waldo was then inserted into different scenes with people surrounding him. The Where's Waldo books were filled with pictures of literally hundreds of people standing very close to each other. Waldo was somewhere in that massive crowd, yet he couldn't easily be seen at first (and maybe second and third) glance.

Many of us walk around like Waldo. We are surrounded by crowds, at the mall, at the grocery store, at a restaurant, and at church. People are all around us, yet we feel like a Waldo—in the middle of a group and yet very alone. Perhaps you've never thought about it this way, but it is possible to be in a place with people all around you and still be lonely.

Country music artist Julie Roberts sings about this on her CD *Men and Mascara*. Lamenting about a relationship that is not fulfilling her needs, she sings about leaving her boyfriend: "I'm already lonely . . . I might as well be lonely alone."[5] Julie's words to her boyfriend echo what many of us are feeling on the inside: we are lonely and feel all alone, regardless of what it looks like to others on the outside. And whether we naively think so or not, a relationship does not cure the lonely factor in our lives.

The truth is we often equate a lonely lifestyle with single women. But I have known plenty of single women who are happily surrounded by caring, godly friends. On the other hand, I've also known married women who feel very, very lonely. We tend to wrongly believe that if we could just get married, our significant other can and will be our all and everything. And sadly, many married women treat their husbands as we do an order of bottomless chips at our favorite restaurant, asking him to continue to fill us up when we are empty.

Even the most logical-thinking women sometimes don't recognize the feeling of loneliness when it happens. We all experience times of loneliness. And we all like to pretend to others that we are completely fulfilled, totally satisfied, and doing just fine without the help of anyone else. But loneliness is an issue that touches our souls and makes us believe that we are uncared for and invisible to others.

> It is possible to be in a place with people all around you and still be lonely.

In case you think that you are alone in your loneliness, let's look at what researchers have uncovered about the epidemic of loneliness in our world today. According to the *Boston Globe*, "Loneliness is becoming a major health problem."[6] A 1990 Gallup study indicated that about 36 percent of Americans are lonely. With an increase in nearly everything else unhealthy in our society, eighteen years later, that statistic has likely gone up.[7]

We really don't need statistics to tell us that we are lonely, do we? Be it demographical in nature—call it a social disability or a major health problem—we are a lonely bunch of women.

And the *Boston Globe* doesn't have to tell us so. Loneliness is an everyday influence in our lives, our decision making, and our portrayal of who we are to others. It's a feeling we try desperately to conceal, preferring to guide others to the belief that we are the last people on earth to ever feel the sting of a lonely night. But who are we kidding, really?

When famed American social writer Eric Hoffer wrote this insightful and interesting quote, I can only imagine the loneliness he himself must have been facing: "It is loneliness that makes the loudest noise. This is true of men as of dogs."[8] (Think of the sound of a howling dog at night.)

Who would have thought that someone who would one day receive the Presidential Medal of Freedom by President Ronald Reagan would experience such loneliness? But just years before his acclaim and successes, Hoffer was an uneducated, homeless man with no family to love him, working on skid row. He tried to enlist in the armed forces but was rejected due to a medical condition. Finally after an unsuccessful suicide attempt, Eric reclaimed his life and found the strength to go on living. It was then that his writing career finally blossomed. But in the meantime, this gifted writer was a very lonely man. And his words certainly reflect that.

> When we find what is worth living for in this life, we discover that anything but very temporary loneliness can't exist in a soul who has found Jesus Christ.

Dag Hammarskjold, winner of the Nobel Peace Prize in 1961, wrote perhaps the most powerful charge to the lonely person yet, in this simple, but eloquent quote: "Pray that your loneliness may spur you into finding something to live for, great enough to die for."

When we find what is worth living for in this life, we discover that anything but very temporary loneliness can't exist in a soul who has found Jesus Christ. Loneliness may make the loudest noise, but it can't hinder the mighty arms of God from reaching down and picking up a broken soul who's all alone in the middle of a lonely night.

FEAR

When I fly, I grip the handles of my airplane chair and pray a lot. People who know me and see me as a strong woman might not expect this to be a fear of mine, but it really is. I do not like to fly, and I get great anxieties over doing it. (Interesting, isn't it, that God would put me on a life journey that requires me to travel!)

I know that fear is not of God . . . in my head. I know that God has not given me the spirit of fear, but of love and of joy and of a sound mind (2 Tim. 1:7). But I have to tell you: my mind doesn't feel very sound when I am thousands of feet in the air! I do not like to know that there are many miles of space between my body and the ground. I do not like the soaring sensation that comes on a plane trip. I do not like the smell of the plane, and I do not like the mini-ature closets they call bathrooms.

Many women get caught up in fear frenzy.

I honestly do not enjoy anything about flying. But it goes a bit further than that, really. It's not simply a dislike—I have a very real *fear* of flying.

The funny thing is you would think that I would have always hated to fly. But I haven't. Up until my midtwenties, I was a frequent flyer, traveling all over the United States for one reason or another. I have flown from coast to coast and many places in between. But somewhere between the Pacific Ocean and Texas, I turned in my wings. And I have never wanted them back.

In the past, my fear of flying kept me from doing some things I wanted to do, like traveling with my husband. After having children, I reasoned that my fear of flying was due to the fact that I did not want to leave them on this earth without a mom, and I did not want to have them with me on a plane if one was going down. Yes, I am afraid to fly, but my fear is not with a plane or in an altitude. If you boil it all down, my fear stems from the feeling of not being able to control something. When I am flying, I feel very out of control.

When we women fear the reactions of others to who we really are, we fear not being able to control the way they feel about us. They might not like us, if they know us. They might not hold us up in high regard or respect us. They might think we are unintelligent or incapable or not able to cope. What we really fear when we pretend to be someone we are not is rejection by others. The fear of rejection often drives us to put on our best game face so that we won't even give someone the chance to think we are *not* all that. Instead, we pretend to be *all that* . . . and then some.

> Our wonderful Savior seeks to comfort us through Scripture when it comes to our fears.

Many women get caught up in fear frenzy. We jump on the bandwagon and embrace the belief system that our every fear is warranted, and we should bring others into the fear-believing fold. Society today encourages us, as women, to fear virtually everything, from communicable diseases (think bird flu) to natural disasters (tsunamis and earthquakes) and terrorism, but it offers no cure for the fearful heart. Meanwhile, we are programmed by society to value virtually nothing in the form of pure living, accurate risk information, and a relationship with God . . . all the things that would help to lessen our fears and stabilize our hearts and minds amid the fearful world we live in.

I wish my fear of flying were the only fear in my life. If I'm honest, I have to admit that I fear other things as well. It's a hard pill for me to swallow to know that at times I am fearful of the rejection of others so much so that I nearly disregard the fact that I am to fear God above all others. Not because He is a mean God but because He is the all-powerful I AM of the universe, who spoke the world into existence . . . and who holds the fate of you and me so carefully in the palm of His hand. Revelation 15:4 reminds us, "Who will not fear you, Lord, and glorify your name? For you alone are holy. All nations will come and worship before you, for your righteous deeds have been revealed" (NLT). We are to fear God in a reverential kind of way because He is . . . well, God.

Our wonderful Savior seeks to comfort us through Scripture when it comes to our fears. He acknowledges that as finite humans, we fear things we shouldn't. But He has compassion on us because He knows we do anyway. The Twenty-third Psalm is a beautiful reminder that fear does not need to rule over us. David writes, "Even when I walk through the darkest valley, I will not be afraid, for you are close beside me" (v. 4 NLT). Even in the face of death, we are not to be afraid, though in our human state, we often are.

Many times we try to control things we are afraid might get out of control. And if they do, we are afraid that we won't be able to handle what happens next. Author and Bible study teacher Beth Moore states it beautifully in her poem "Holding Us":

We often see ourselves as fragile, breakable souls
We live in fear of that which we are certain
    we can't survive.

As children of God, we are only as fragile as our
    unwillingness to hide our face in Him.
Our pride alone is fragile.
Once its shell is broken and the heart laid bare,
We can sense the caress of God's tender care.
Until then He holds us just the same.[9]

Whether we are feeling insecure, jealous, lonely, or afraid, our precious Father desires to hold us and tell us we are worthy, important, gifted, never alone, and never to fear. He longs to uncover these feelings we hide so that we can find out who we are, once and for all . . . without all the concealer.

part three

THE REAL DEAL

eight

WE ARE COMPLETELY LOVED AND ACCEPTED COMPLETELY

*How great is the love the Father
has lavished on us, that we should be called
children of God! And that is what we are!*
—1 JOHN 3:1

My friend Christa has a great sense of humor and can always make me laugh. She is not a joke-telling kind of girl, but she has a dry, sarcastic wit, and I love that. She consoles me when I am complaining about having eaten one too many brownies by responding, "Oh, didn't you hear? Fat grams don't count on Fridays!" She has been known to tell me a time or two that I am so skinny she can hardly see me. (It's a lie, but I don't care!) It brings a smile to my face every time she leaves me a message on my voice mail by singing, "What a friend I have in Lisa" (to the tune of the wonderful hymn . . . no blasphemy intended!) . . . always at the right time, it seems, in the midst of a crazy day. I love my friend.

Christa also has a phrase she uses when she sees me discouraged about something. She will smile and say, "You know, Lisa, it will be okay. Remember, you are an awesome spirit being, truly loved and accepted by God." This is a well-known phrase from an even-better-known book, *The Search for Significance*.[1] In fact, she says it quite often and quite fast, and it has become a kind of mantra for us during tough times. And it is the perfect way to open this section of the book as we look at the *real deal* about who we truly are.

WE ARE COMPLETELY LOVED

The depth of God's love for us is hard to comprehend. So are the height, the width, and the breadth of His love. Our human minds will not allow us to process the greatness of the love of our Father because we are programmed by the world's view of love, which has great limitations. The handbook of worldly love outlines for us some guidelines we must follow in order to ever find it. Things like, *Remember that love is just a feeling . . . If you love someone, let him go . . . Recognize that you are the biggest love of your own life . . .* Nice captions for greeting cards but hardly the gospel truth.

A couple of years ago, I was visiting with a longtime friend. She had been through some difficult years and a few bad relationships and was reflecting on her experiences. I was listening closely to her, trying to interject some nuggets of wisdom every now and then when I heard her say these words: "I really want to experience true love again. You know, the kind

> The depth of God's love for us is hard to comprehend.

of love that makes you a better person. If there's one thing I've learned through all of this, it's that true love should never hurt. I guess that's why they say, 'Love is never having to say I'm sorry.'" When I heard her say that, I nearly choked. I couldn't believe someone so intelligent, capable, and insightful could actually repeat such nonsense! *No wonder her relationships have not lasted*, I thought. *At least in my house, love is always having to say I'm sorry since I so often mess up!*

My dear friend is not alone in her thoughts on love. In researching this subject, I came across quote after quote and poem after poem about the way we, as the world, view love. Here is one such person's view, posted on the Web in a poem entitled "What Is It That I Love?"

> If asked why I love her I would say
> It's the sway in her hips,
> the thickness in her thighs.
> It's the lust in her lips,
> the love in her eyes.
> It's the softness of her skin,
> the silk in her hair.
> It's the twist in her walk;
> it's the sweetness in her talk.
> It's the way she loves me
> that makes me love her each day.
> That is what I would say.[2]

While I do not personally know the man who wrote this and certainly cannot judge his relationships or his heart, I am slightly dismayed by his words. I fear this is the lens much of the world is looking through to form our opinions about love—a physical attraction and a perceived admiration. If this is our view of love, no wonder we are no good at it.

And we can't blame it on our age or lack of knowing better. Even middle-aged women with good life experience under our belts are falling for the world's view of love. We look to celebrities, romance novels, and reality TV to define our standards for love, and then we wonder why those voted most likely to succeed in society never experience any love that is long-lasting. We search the Internet for connections with people who have no more of a clue about love than we do! Yet we think that one more click of a button will bring us the lasting love we have been seeking. Sadly, we couldn't be more disillusioned.

I read a story once about a man and his wife who were visiting an orphanage where they hoped to adopt a child. In an interview with the boy they wanted to adopt, they told him in glowing terms about the many things they could give him. To their amazement, the little guy said, "If you have nothing to offer except a good home, clothes, toys, and the other things that most kids have—why, I would just as soon stay here." Puzzled, the woman asked, "What on earth could you want besides those things?" The boy replied, "I just want someone to love me."

That's what we all really want, isn't it? Deep down inside, when no one is around and the only sound that breaks the silence is the beating of our own hearts, we long to feel the warm embrace of love wrapped around us. We desire to truly experience lasting and genuine love, maybe for the first time in our lives. What we thought would bring us love has let us down, and we are tired of searching. Even the best of our earthly relationships with the strongest bonds of earthly love cannot quench the insatiable thirst of our souls for a deeper connection . . . so much so that we're not even sure anymore that it really exists.

One of my favorite gospel groups of all time is BeBe and CeCe Winans. Their music has ministered to my heart on many occasions, and I love the poignancy of the lyrics to their songs. One of their CDs I love the most is *Different Lifestyles*. It was released in 1991 when I was in my junior year of college, and it quickly became my CD of choice. I listened to it over and over that year, maybe hundreds of times. My college roommates grew so tired of hearing it they almost banned it . . . and me . . . from the room. But I never got tired of playing it.

One song in particular touched my heart. It's a song cowritten by BeBe called "Searching for Love (It's Real)." The melody of the song is rich and beautiful, and it meant a great deal to me during that year in college when I was doing a lot of my own searching for love. While the message of the song is deep and meaningful, the opening lyrics of the song start out very simply by posing a question: "Searching for love . . . has anyone found it?" And then the song goes on to describe how people search for love, sometimes for a lifetime, without ever really discovering it. And it talks about how much it hurts when we keep looking, never to find anything real . . . anyone real . . . who will love us, truly love us. That is, except for One.[3]

The good news of that song is the same good news of this book. Someone does love us. He tells us so in one of my favorite verses in the entire Bible: "I have loved you with an everlasting love" (Jer. 31:3). I feel that verse down to my very toes every time I read it because its message never changes, and its promise is so completely thorough. God's love is without pretense, without conditions, and without limits. His love feels good the night before, the morning after, and every time in between. It is like water to a thirsty soul, food to a hungry heart, and freedom to a confined prisoner. It is nothing short of amazing, and I am constantly amazed by it. I cannot believe He loves me like He does . . . and He loves you just the same.

The poet Robert Frost once said, "Love is an irresistible desire to be irresistibly desired." Whether we desire Him or not, we are irresistibly desired by God. He overwhelms us with His love in His flood of love letters to us, so much so that we could fill large spans of time simply reading about it. Only the great Lover of our souls could capture our hearts with such beautiful words as these:

- ✦ The LORD will command His lovingkindness in the daytime, and in the night His song shall be with me— a prayer to the God of my life. (Ps. 42:8 NKJV)
- ✦ The LORD your God is with you, he is mighty to save. He will take great delight in you, he will quiet you with his love. (Zeph. 3:17)
- ✦ For I am convinced that neither death nor life, neither angels nor demons, neither the present nor the future, nor any powers, neither height nor depth, nor anything else in all creation, will be able to separate us from the love of God that is in Christ Jesus our Lord. (Rom. 8:38–39)
- ✦ That Christ may dwell in your hearts through faith; that you, being rooted and grounded in love, may be able to comprehend with all the saints what is the width and length and depth and height—to know the

love of Christ which passes knowledge; that you may
be filled with all the fullness of God. (Eph. 3:17–19
NKJV)

Ironically, the vibrant love of God, which colors our very
soul and breathes life in us, always leads us back to Jesus'
death on the cross so many years ago. Need reminding?
"Greater love has no one than this, that he lay down his life
for his friends" (John 15:13). Rest assured that no one has
ever loved us more than He does. Romans 5:8 says, "God
demonstrates his own love for us in this: While we were still
sinners, Christ died for us." Even when we were the most
unattractive, God showed us just how much He loved us.
And He loves us still, even in our curlers and terry-cloth
bathrobes, unsightly to anyone else but Him.

The reality is that many of us have known about God's love
for a long, long time. Perhaps the most familiar verse in all of
the Bible is one we memorized as a child: "For God so loved the
world that he gave his one and
only Son, that whoever believes in
him shall not perish but have eternal life" (John 3:16). The difference in the way we see that verse
now is the difference between head
knowledge and heart knowledge.
Even if we learned this verse in our younger years, it does not
guarantee that the truth has ever really registered. No, the
familiarity of that verse does not truly represent its status in our
minds and, more importantly, in our hearts.

> God's love is without
> pretense, without
> conditions, and
> without limits.

In his book *Above All*, author Brennan Manning recounts
his experience of being changed forever by an encounter with

God in a seminary chapel. Having known *about* Christ for years prior, he tells of his first real heart experience with His Creator. In a chapter he titles "The Furious Love of Christ," Manning soulfully writes:

> In my first-ever experience of being loved for nothing I had done or could do, I moved back and forth between mild ecstasy, silent wonder, and hushed trembling. The aura might be best described as "bright darkness." The moment lingered on in a timeless now, until without warning I felt a hand grip my heart. It was abrupt and startling. The awareness of being loved was no longer tender and comforting. The love of Christ, the crucified Son of God, took on the wild fury of a sudden spring storm. Like a dam bursting, a spasm of convulsive crying erupted from the depths of my soul. *Jesus died on the cross for me.* I had known that since grade school, in the way of what John Henry Newman called "notional knowledge"—abstract, far away, irrelevant to the gut issues of life, another trinket in the dusty pawnshop of doctrinal beliefs. But in one blinding moment of salvific truth, it became real knowledge calling for personal engagement of my heart. Christianity was no longer merely a moral code, an ethic, or a philosophy of life but a love affair. At last, drained, spent, and lost in speechless humility, I was back kneeling at the seashore with gentle waves of love sweeping over me, saturating my mind and heart in a quiet, unselfconscious mode of silent adoration.[4]

Manning's words strike a chord in my heart. If you've ever felt truly and completely loved by God, you know how God's love is fantastic and furious at the same time. It is strong, and it is swift. It is a heavenly wonder, unmatched by anything earthly. And when you experience it in your heart, it makes it impossible to settle for love of any other kind.

There's a familiar story in the Bible that perfectly illustrates the gracious love of God. It's found in chapter 4 of the gospel of John. Jesus was on His way back to Galilee, after being in Judea. Instead of going out of His way to walk around Samaria, which was an unpopular place for Jews to travel due to stringent cultural restrictions, the Bible tells us that Jesus "had to go through Samaria" (v. 4). Although Jesus was a Jew, He traveled through Samaria, despite the cultural taboo of doing so.

> The reality is that many of us have known about God's love for a long, long time.

Tired and thirsty from His journey, Jesus came across a well and stopped beside it. It was almost noontime, a time that the customary well drawers were not usually there. On this day, however, there was a woman . . . the Bible does not mention her by name, but it tells us that she was from Samaria. She had come to draw water, and she happened upon Jesus. But there was no coincidence about their meeting.

"Will you give me a drink?" (v. 7) Jesus asked the woman. She was surprised. She did not expect such a request from a Jewish man. Pointing out the obvious differences between them, the Samaritan woman asked Jesus why He would ask her for a drink. He replied, "If you knew the gift of God and who it is that asks you for a drink, you would have asked him, and he would have given you living water" (v. 10). Jesus knew that she had no idea to whom she was talking. But He wanted her to know. And He wanted her to experience the unconditional love of another for the first time in her life because she had been looking for love a long time, just in all the wrong places.

The Samaritan woman had been married five times and was living with yet another man when she met Christ this divinely appointed day at the well. Because of His divinity, He already knew this about her—and He wanted her to know He knew. His desire was for her to finally look into the eyes of Someone who wanted nothing from her but had everything to offer her.

> All Jesus wanted to do was give her the gift of love she hadn't been able to find in anything or anyone else.

After the Samaritan woman questioned Jesus' ability to provide her with living water, He lovingly addressed her concerns: "Everyone who drinks this water will be thirsty again, but whoever drinks the water I give him will never thirst . . . [It] will become in him a spring of water welling up to eternal life" (vv. 13–14). He couldn't have made it clearer. Jesus' love was the only answer for her thirsty heart. She didn't have to have a proper pedigree, and her past was of no eternal importance. All Jesus wanted to do was give her the gift of love she hadn't been able to find in anything or anyone else. And like so many of us, she had certainly tried.

WE ARE ACCEPTED COMPLETELY

Have you ever stopped to think about the fact that God knows your favorite color of Skittles? Hardly a profound thought, I know, but a true statement nonetheless. And a more important one than you might at first think.

Just recently, my six-year-old son, Micah, and I were enjoying a few minutes together. For a special treat, I was letting him eat his favorite candy, Skittles. We were having a nice mommy-son moment, and before I knew it, he was sharing his Skittles with me. This was no small thing since he loves Skittles more than most anything else in the world, at least, more than any other candy. First, he picked a yellow one out of the bowl. Then he gave me an orange one. And then he sorted through them and carefully picked out a purple one. I noticed that his choices seemed deliberate—he was picking out my favorite ones. After a moment or two, I said to him, "Micah, how do you know which ones I like?" since I didn't ever remember having that conversation with him before. And with all the innocence in the world, he looked up at me and said plainly, "'Cause you're my mom."

> God has done things to show us His unconditional acceptance of us like none other ever has or ever will.

No flowery answer. No long speech. Just a simple explanation that meant so much. A deeper translation of his four-word answer would be something like, "No duh, Mom. I don't need any other reason to know what you like or don't like. Our relationship is reason enough!" His acceptance of what should have been obvious to me made me a little envious of his youthful wisdom.

Acceptance from God works the same way. It is not necessary to be intellectualized or analyzed. It is what it is. Simple in concept, yet there is nothing ordinary about it. And it's marvelous beyond words.

God has done things to show us His unconditional acceptance of us like none other ever has or ever will. Rest assured that Someone who would go to the trouble of counting the number of hairs on your head (Matt. 10:30) loves you entirely and accepts you completely, with sheer abandon. And He knows and cares about the smallest things, even your favorite color of Skittles.

Oh, if we would only recognize our heritage. He is our Dad. You and I were accepted into the family without a clause in our contract. Hosea 2:19 says, "I will betroth you to me forever; I will betroth you in righteousness and justice, in love and compassion." Our birth certificate has been stamped with a seal of authenticity as a child of God, and He is never giving us back or letting us go.

Verses about God's deep concern toward us remind us of His precious and complete acceptance of us:

- ✤ Cast all your anxiety on him because he cares for you. (1 Peter 5:7)
- ✤ Before I formed you in the womb I knew you, before you were born I set you apart. (Jer. 1:5)
- ✤ You know me, O LORD; you see me. (Jer. 12:3)
- ✤ You understand, O LORD; remember me and care for me. (Jer. 15:15)
- ✤ Come near to God and he will come near to you. (James 4:8)
- ✤ I will not leave you comfortless: I will come to you. (John 14:18 KJV)
- ✤ And my God will meet all your needs according to his glorious riches in Christ Jesus. (Phil. 4:19)

I remember well my beloved late grandfather singing, "Bless the Lord, O my soul, and all that is within me, bless His holy name." He was professing his gratitude for how God had always loved and accepted him and how He was caring for him, even into his latter years. Psalm 103:2–4 says, "Praise the LORD, O my soul, and forget not all his benefits—who forgives all your sins and heals all your diseases, who redeems your life from the pit and crowns you with love and compassion."

Our heavenly Father has done such an enormous thing for us by loving us, accepting us, and adopting us into His family! He talks about our deed of inheritance in verses from the Old Testament to the New, and in the book of Romans He makes it crystal clear: "For his Holy Spirit speaks to us deep in our hearts, and tells us that we really are God's children. And since we are his children, we will share his treasures— for all God gives to his Son Jesus is now ours too" (8:16–17 TLB). It's party time, ladies! We are His kids!

When my daughter was three, she and I did something that held meaning only for the two of us. It's something she transitioned out of as she got older, sooner than her senti- mental mom wanted. But while she did indulge me, I milked it for all it was worth. It was a very simple back-and-forth banter between us in which I would ask her, "Are you gonna be my baby princess?" And she would grin and giggle and run around the room on her tiny little legs while I chased her like a crazy person, asking over and over, "Are you or not? Will you be my baby princess or not?" And we would laugh and laugh until we'd both collapse on the floor, and I would hold her close and look into her blue-green eyes. Finally, after what seemed like hours, she would say the one word I was longing to hear from her . . . "Yes." And it is as if I couldn't breathe until she confirmed to me what I already knew to be true . . . that she was *mine*.

Our precious heavenly Father feels that way about us. He's omniscient, so He already knows that we are His, if we have accepted Him into our hearts; but He wants to hear us acknowledge it in our hearts and to ourselves. God already knows that He accepts us just as we are . . . with all of our failures and faults and insecurities, but He wants *us* to know that—to *really* know that. He's written us love letter after love letter in His Holy Word, the Bible, but we still sometimes have

> Our heavenly Father has done such an enormous thing for us by loving us, accepting us, and adopting us into His family!

a hard time grasping the fact that we are accepted totally . . . completely, truly, and 100 percent accepted. Though He has proven to us time and again that even when we mess up He doesn't stop loving and accepting us, we still seek His approval. And we still long to hear Him tell us over and over again that we are His—His precious baby princesses.

It's hard for most, if not all of us, to realize that God's acceptance of us is not like the acceptance (or lack thereof) we get from our worldly relationships. The truth is we never totally feel accepted every day by anyone on this earth, even the people who love and care for us the very most. We often feel judged and compromised by the people around us, and we just can't seem to shake the feeling that God also somehow reserves His opinion of us, depending upon how we behave or what we say and do. We fear that the jury may be still out about us, and the Judge hasn't had His final say.

It never ceases to amaze me how God pauses every now and then to show me in a divine way that His acceptance of me is a nonissue. If given the opportunity, I feel sure that many of you could share stories of when God delivered a message to you about where you stood with Him. One such time happened to me about six months ago on a sleepy Monday morning. But let me start with what happened on Sunday night.

It was a typical e-mail from a friend. Actually, nothing about the friend or the e-mail was typical. The truth is that I had been having some conflict with my friend, so much so that I had been considering severing our relationship but had not had the courage to do so. Her e-mail was about an issue that was very dear to my heart, and what she wrote bothered me a great deal. She was giving me her opinion about something I firmly disagreed with, and I was feeling very judged by her about it. I left the computer that night discouraged, defeated, and disappointed. Score one for Satan.

I went upstairs to engage in my usual bedtime routine of makeup removal, teeth brushing, and contact lens cleaning when I decided to take a minute to call the one person in the world I believed could make me feel better . . . my precious and godly mother. She answered, and we talked . . . or at least, I talked at her. She listened and then spoke. Steadily and wisely, she shared her insights into what she felt was happening. "I really think this is Satan trying to get to you, Lisa. He is using this issue to make you feel judged and wrong and misguided. Please don't allow him to convince you of something that is not true." More conversation followed, and after a lot of tears and a good dose of wisdom from Mom, we said good night. "I'll be praying for you, honey," she told me.

> God already knows that He accepts us just as we are . . . with all of our failures and faults and insecurities, but He wants us to know that— to really know that.

After reassuring my husband that I was not having a nervous breakdown (I am not usually much of a crier), I slipped under the covers and looked at the ceiling. *God*, I prayed silently, *please show me that I am okay with You. I really just want to know we are tracking.* With that, I turned over and closed my eyes. Sleep came quickly.

I awoke the next morning, earlier than usual. It was still dark outside, and my alarm clock hadn't even sounded. But I was definitely awake—in a really strange way. I had a song in my head that was playing like a tape being rewound and played and rewound and played again. This was unusual for me, on many levels. For one thing, anyone who knows me will testify to the fact that I am not a morning person. And I am certainly not a morning person who wakes up without an alarm and humming a song. Not on any typical day, at least.

I quickly made my way downstairs, determining to write down the words to this song before I forgot them, still having no idea where I had heard the song or why I was singing it. In my semi-foggy state, I located a notebook in a cabinet drawer in my kitchen and wrote down the words that were in my mind. I scribbled down the date, shut the notebook, and headed to the coffeepot to start brewing a fresh batch for my still-sleeping husband and myself. It wasn't even 6:00 a.m.

The day held its usual routine of carpooling, grocery shopping, and dish washing after dinner. I had almost forgotten about the song in my notebook, had it not been for my husband's question after we got the kids to bed and were finally able to catch up about our day. "Why were you up so early this morning? You beat me up." Scotty is an early bird, and he is almost always out of bed before I am. "Oh, I don't know. I just couldn't sleep, I guess," I said. It was then that I remembered the real reason I was up early . . . the song I couldn't shake. I couldn't even remember what the words were, so I was glad I had written them down.

"I'll be back in a minute, okay?" I left my husband with a promise to continue our conversation shortly. He agreed, and I made my way downstairs to the closed notebook lying on the counter. Opening it, I was surprised at how clearly I had written the words, since I could hardly remember writing them at all. I read:

> Clean, before my Lord
> I stand, and in me, not one blemish
> Does He see.
> When I place all my burdens on Him,
> He washes them all from me.[5]

The simplicity of the words ministered to my heart, and I knew all at once that God had spoken to me . . . clearly, specifically, and loudly. *We are okay, Lisa. We are tracking.* I heard His message to me in a very bold and powerful way. I was accepted by Him. I was not being judged by my Creator, but rather, I was loved. I felt His love and acceptance in five short phrases of a song I couldn't remember ever hearing. Yet I could hear it in my head as if it were a song I knew very well. Out of all He had going on that Monday morning, my heavenly Father had paused long enough to reach down from heaven and pick up my sad heart to hold in His hands. The moment was very real. And I was ever so grateful.

Several weeks later I was cleaning out some drawers in the kitchen when I ran across the notebook I had hardly thought about since that Monday. I opened it once again and read the words to the mystery song I woke up singing not long before. *Where in the world have I heard that song?* I thought. *I know I've heard it before, but I don't remember when! Yet it's so familiar to me.*

That's when it dawned on me. The song I could barely remember as a thirty-four-year-old was a song I used to listen to by an artist I deeply loved as a child. Her name was Evie. She had snow-white hair and an angelic voice. I loved her, and I loved her music. I could hardly believe it. I hadn't heard her music for almost twenty-six years since I no longer owned an eight-track or record player. I was just a child when I had her album . . . barely eight years old. I didn't know where the album was or even what the name of the song was. I could only remember that one short verse and the way she sang it.

The voice I heard that Monday morning was not the voice of Evie but the glorious voice of God, serenading me with His Spirit. I cried at the awesome lengths He had gone to work out this divine moment, just to show me He and I were okay. That we were tracking. *What an amazing heavenly Dad I have.*

nine

WE ARE COMPLETELY FLAWED
YET FORGIVEN COMPLETELY

*Oh, what joy for those whose disobedience
is forgiven, whose sins are put out of sight.*

— ROMANS 4:7 NLT

Before Scotty and I married, we attended ten weeks of pre-marital counseling. It was a positive experience for us as we gleaned a great deal of wisdom and insight into what married life would be like from our counselor, Dr. Dan. After twelve years of marriage, we still recall much of what he taught us about what to do and more importantly, what not to do in our relationship.

One of the things Dr. Dan said stuck with me, and I think of it quite often when my husband and I have a fight or a disagreement. Dr. Dan wisely suggested that when in an argument with your spouse, you should avoid using absolutes, such as, "You *never* take out the trash!" . . . or "You *always* start a fight with my mother!". . . or "You won't *ever* change!" Even though I acknowledge that he is right, I almost wish Dr. Dan hadn't told us this because it seems as though I constantly have to change my verbiage to meet with his counsel. After all, it's really hard not to use words like *never* and *always* when you are fighting passionately with your spouse about things you are convinced deserve such strong and definitive language!

But now I understand better why he would suggest refraining from casual usage of these kinds of absolute statements—because they are often inaccurate and usually overstated and can probably be refuted at one point or another.

> We are flawed and forgiven all at the same time.

But in contrast, the principle I want to show you in this chapter isn't inaccurate, isn't overstated, and cannot be refuted. It's an absolute truth that is absolutely amazing. It's the truth that we women, as people and as followers of Christ, are completely flawed and yet forgiven completely.

Totally . . . wholly . . . entirely . . . fully . . . utterly . . . absolutely . . . from top to bottom . . . from tip to toe . . . completely. Leaving nothing out and overstating nothing. We are flawed and forgiven all at the same time. And not just partially forgiven. We are sinful, down to our very core, and we are sanctified, down to our very soul.

And though we'd like to, we can't accept only the good part of this equation (that we are forgiven completely), leaving out the part we don't particularly like (that we are completely flawed). It can't work that way, and here's the reason: because being completely fleshly and flawed from top to bottom and from tip to toe makes room for us to be forgiven in an entirely equal way. And knowing that makes the beauty of the completeness of the act of forgiveness by almighty God that much more meaningful and incredible and *real* in our lives.

WE ARE COMPLETELY FLAWED

Like all moms, I have had mornings I would like to erase, rewind, or do over. This was one such morning when anything and everything had gone seriously wrong, and I was at my wits' end.

I awoke to a finger poking me in my side. "Yes, honey. What is it?" I cracked one eye open just enough to see a tiny figure, dressed in pink flannel, with mounds of curly hair, standing next to my side of the bed. "I pee-peed in my bed, Mommy. I all wet." I closed my eye again, silently hoping that when I opened it again, my daughter would be sleeping soundly in her bed instead of standing next to mine. But the voice was persistent. "Mom-mee! Wake up! *I all wet!*" I reluctantly pulled the warm covers off of me and got out of bed, bemoaning the fact that I had to change my daughter's sheets for the third night in a row . . . none too pleased at the abrupt way my much-needed sleep had been interrupted. Little did I know this was only the beginning of a morning that was going to be anything but perfect.

After stripping the wet sheets off the bed and getting my daughter settled into clean panties and pajamas, I made my way downstairs to the coffeepot. The usual smell of coffee did not welcome me, which meant that my usually dependable husband had not started the coffee for me before he left for his meeting at work. Bummer! I stared at the coffeepot for several seconds before realizing that I needed to do something to meet my need for coffee. And on this morning, believe me, I needed it.

Opening up the cabinet door, I realized why my husband had not prepared the coffee—we were out. Nearing a lack-of-caffeine breakdown, I opted instead for the cold counterpart to my coffee—a can of Diet Coke—and I continued with my usual routine. After pulling myself together enough to go to my son's preschool, I then moved on to the task of readying my son for the day. He was upset by my shirt choice for him because it didn't "feel good," so I provided him with several other options to avoid further meltdown. Settling on one, we moved on to the pants, only to discover the ones my son wanted to wear were in the washing machine and could not be dried in time. Things were not going well.

In the midst of the clothes chaos, the phone rang, and I ran to get it. My husband was on the line: "Hey, honey. Did you remember that the cable guy is coming between 8 a.m. and noon to hook up our DIRECTV?" I couldn't get the words out to protest (good thing probably, especially since I was about to tell him that I couldn't possibly remember something that was never previously told to me) before the sound of the doorbell chimed throughout the house. *Oh, great,* I thought. *Can't wait to see the cable guy.* I mumbled a quick, "Gotta go," to my husband and ran to the door. By the look on his face, the cable guy was as excited to see me as I was to see him.

After giving the installer strict instructions to "please hurry," I resumed my parental duties. My now-throbbing head required Advil. Making my way back upstairs, I spotted a trail of salmon-colored dots leading me to the room where the children were watching TV. The dots culminated into a massive spot right next to an empty princess juice cup, the culprit of the leak. Irritated, I spouted off at my baby girl, still oblivious to any kind of problem. "Shae! Why didn't you tell Mommy your juice was leaking? You've made a mess all over the carpet!" Looking down at the carpet, the realization finally set in for my precious child; she looked at me and said, "Oh, sowwee, Mommy. I sowwee I spiwwed it." I sighed and then got on my hands and knees and scrubbed the stains away.

After finally getting rid of the cable guy, cleaning the carpet, and making sure everyone had on clothes and shoes, I glanced at my daily planner to double-check my schedule. To my horror, I read the words *Dentist Appointment—9:30 a.m.* and nearly ran to my room to have the same meltdown my son had previously had this morning. How could I have overlooked that appointment? But I had. And I was running very late, so it would be a miracle if I made it on time.

When I was finally ready to head out the door, my daughter dropped another bombshell on me. "Mommy, I don't want my Pop Tarts. They're yucky!"

Now at my breaking point, I mumbled something about how she could do this to me and why she had picked this morning to inform me that the Pop Tarts she normally loved and asked to eat every morning were now incompatible to her tiny taste buds. "What do you want then, Shae?" I asked. Her response came quickly. "Can I have some chips?" With no time or energy left to argue, I grabbed a snack-sized bowl of chips and shoved them at her. "Here. Now let's go!"

The car ride was quiet, except for the sound of my husband's wooden coat hanger he had left in the back clanging and clinking with every turn of the car. It was just one more reminder to me of how annoyed I was and how bad my day was going. We pulled into the school, and I ordered the kids out of the car. My daughter still needed help with her car-seat belt, so I came around to her side to unhook her. "Mommy, can I bring my chips in?" Shae asked. It was not a school day for her, but I knew the other mothers dropping off kids would be around. I was definitely not wanting to offer any explanations of why my three-year-old had chips at nine in the morning, but I also didn't want to mess with trying to take them away from her either. The scales were pretty even, so I reluctantly agreed.

Making our way inside, we arrived at my son's classroom, where his teacher greeted us. "Good morning, Micah. How are you this morning?" Micah mustered a grin and entered the room. I was so glad she hadn't asked me that. "Wait, buddy. Can I have a kiss?" I asked. I didn't want to leave him at school without him feeling love from me . . . and I needed it too! Without hesitation, he ran back over to me and gave me a huge bear hug and slobbery kiss. Just the medicine I needed!

I had turned my back on Shae to say good-bye to Micah and to chat with the teacher for a minute. I knew the Valentine's party was right around the corner, and I needed to sign up to bring something. As the teacher and I talked, I could hear a crunching noise, at first subtly, then loudly, right behind me. I turned around just in time to see Shae, stepping on chips that were now in at least a zillion pieces on the floor in front of her. An empty bowl sat facedown on the floor right beside her.

"Shae Elisabeth," I snarled through clenched teeth. "What in the world do you think you are doing?" She stopped her stomping, but said no words. The answer was quite obvious. "Sowwee, Mommy," she finally said. As the mothers maneuvered their way through the chip-laden floor, I got some sympathetic glances, some humored glances, and some scrutinizing glances. Already feeling judged for allowing my daughter to have chips for breakfast, I quickly picked up the chip pieces that were big enough to grab.

Looking back at the teacher, I could only come up with two words to utter on this morning that had gone awry to explain my child's poor behavior . . . I shrugged my shoulders and said, "Sin nature." She laughed and I cringed as I let the reality of those two words set in. I wasn't trying to be poetic or deeply spiritual—it was just the first thought that popped into my head to describe the situation. But upon later reflection, I knew it wasn't a coincidence that God had impressed upon me those particular words . . . and although I thought it was about my daughter's actions, the truth is that it was the truth about *me*.

We are all what I call *perfectly imperfect*. In other words, we were each born with a sin nature that often controls us and leads us to do things that go against what we really want to do. The apostle Paul details his own struggle with the sin nature in his letter to the Romans, where he so plainly yet eloquently writes,

> I don't understand myself at all, for I really want to do what is right, but I can't. I do what I don't want to—what I hate. I know perfectly well that what I am doing is wrong, and my bad conscience proves that I agree with these laws I am breaking. But I can't help myself, because I'm no longer doing it. It is sin inside me that is stronger than I am that makes me do these evil things. I know I am rotten through and through so far as my old sinful nature is concerned. No matter which way I turn I can't make myself do right. I want to but I can't. (7:15–18 TLB)

Paul continues, expressing his frustration with himself:

When I want to do good, I don't; and when I try not to do wrong, I do it anyway. Now if I am doing what I don't want to, it is plain where the trouble is: sin still has me in its evil grasp. It seems to be a fact of life that when I want to do what is right, I inevitably do what is wrong. (vv. 19–21 TLB)

Then as if he suddenly gains some clarity into his struggle, Paul gives himself a small break. "I love God's law with all my heart. But there is another law at work within me that is at war with my mind. This law wins the fight and makes me a slave to the sin that is still within me" (vv. 22–23 NLT). His agony is apparent as he further bares his soul: "Oh, what a miserable person I am! Who will free me from this life that is dominated by sin?" (v. 24 NLT).

Already knowing the answer to his own question, Paul sums up his musings in the last verse of the chapter: "Thank God! The answer is in Jesus Christ our Lord. So you see how it is: In my mind I really want to obey God's law, but because of my sinful nature I am a slave to sin" (v. 25 NLT).

> We are all what I call *perfectly imperfect.*

As Paul is pointing out to us through this powerful passage, our sin nature at times enslaves and dominates us. Please don't misunderstand me. It's not that we can't do right or that we are helpless victims to our sinful nature, but if we do not allow ourselves to be controlled by the Holy Spirit, our sin nature takes over. And that's when things get really messy.

Whether it is reckless behavior, a mischievous action like

my daughter's stomping chips, or a bad attitude like I had on a morning that was not going my way, it's human nature to act in ways that are irresponsible, rude, negative, destructive, and ungodly. Even when we are the best self we can ever be in our own strength, we are still influenced by our fleshly and sinful tendencies.

I recently attended a conference for writers and speakers. It was a helpful and positive experience, and the hosts of the conference did a great job promoting sincerity and sisterly love and encouragement among the participants. Though there were several hundred women in attendance with similar goals in mind, there was a sweet spirit present, and it provided for me a picture of what I consider edification at its best. Despite the different levels of success among the participants—some having book contracts and some wanting them . . . some having solidly developed speaking platforms and established ministries and some simply feeling a nudge from God to share a message He put on their hearts—everyone in attendance encouraged one another, prayed for one another, and focused on others' strengths, rather than their weaknesses. I left the conference feeling convinced in my calling and endorsed by my peers as I suspect most everyone did.

> If we do not allow ourselves to be controlled by the Holy Spirit, our sin nature takes over. And that's when things get really messy.

But my experience at this conference, though extremely positive, confirmed something in my heart I already knew about myself but didn't like to admit: even at our best, we are not quite good enough. Despite the fact that at a conference like that, everyone feels called by God and is genuinely joyful about how God is working in the lives of others, there is still the nature within us that wants to have and be more than those around us. We are fleshly and flawed; no matter how truly happy we are for someone else, the raw and ugly truth is that we would be happier for ourselves. We can rejoice when someone gets a book contract or a big speaking engagement, a fatter paycheck or a newer car, a bigger house or a better-looking spouse, a more-accomplished child or a more-toned body . . . but if we were to be honest, we would admit that we want it more for ourselves. Why? It's in our nature.

Sometimes we don't even hide it that well. If this conference were edification at its best, then a beauty pageant would have to represent edification at its worst. If you don't believe me, watch the next one that comes on TV and draw your own conclusions. And while I am sure not all pageant contestants are like the ones we see in the movie *Miss Congeniality*, I think you will come to understand and possibly appreciate my point after you hear what I am saying. Here's the scenario.

After pasting on freshly whitened smiles, the participants can hardly hide their anxiety as the top ten are called. One by one the camera scans the beauties as a select few hear their names and show visible relief, knowing they will be allowed to continue in the contest. They each react in different ways— some with a pumped fist in the air, some with open arms and a *thank you* mouthed to the judges, some hugging the persons next to them with tears in their eyes—before taking their places in the semicircle on the dot appointed to them. But all ten are apparently very delighted at making it through one more cut. The other contestants? Not so much.

By the time the top five picks are chosen, the other contestants have recovered enough to perform the highly choreographed dance routine they are required to do at the end of the program. Now five other hopeful girls' dreams are crushed, and they are whisked off the stage as though they have just been "gonged." Still smiling, they relent.

The big moment has finally arrived. After answering the one final question of the night and with one more commercial break, the names of the finalists are called. Five . . . four . . . and three are called, leading up to the real moment everyone is interested in. Only two girls are left, and they are now clutching each other's hands as if they have been lifelong friends rather than competitors, both of them already in tears. The first runner-up is announced. Though the winner's name has yet to be called, in an effort to capture her reaction, the camera pans quickly to her. She squeals . . . she screams . . . she cries . . . she shakes . . . she thanks both her supporters and judges though her words can't be heard over the cheer of the crowd . . . and she accepts her crown and roses as the newly minted winner.

> Even at our best, we are not quite good enough.

Picture-perfect, the newly crowned beauty queen makes her way down the runway to the theme song of choice. Her smiles and waves continue, despite the fact that she is probably really uncomfortable in her skintight dress and wants to peel off her double-sided tape and just go have a burger and fries! But she feels the call to duty as her reign has just begun, and she is fully in the moment of realizing what may well have been a lifelong dream. Then, having finished her runway walk and in a final act of her crowning, she makes her way up to the very top of the stage, past all of the nonwinning contestants. And that's when the real stuff happens.

If the women were previously entering the stage one by one, now they are flocking to the winner in large numbers as she sits on her perch with a glistening crown. A sea of multicolored and bejeweled gowns rushes to her, congratulating her with hugs and kisses and well wishes. In an alleged moment of rejoicing, the winner's crown gets knocked off, and her sash falls off her shoulder, and the red lip prints on her face are being worked on by at least four different women, trying to remove the smudges they have left behind. By the time the telecast goes off, the winner is seen trying to hold it together or, at least, hold it all on, and the real show has now been seen.

Though I still enjoy watching a pageant now and then, I have to admit that in my many years of pageant watching, I have often wondered what those last few moments were really all about. Were the women sincerely happy for the winner? Did they *accidentally* knock her crown off in the middle of congratulating her? Or did they really just want a second more of camera time to show off the dress, hair, and makeup they paid a fortune for and maybe somehow make the winner look a bit less attractive to the people who just voted her the best woman for the job? Call me a skeptic, but these women have been training, tanning, lifting, spraying, sweating, and practicing for months and even years in preparation for this event, and we are supposed to believe that they are truly *happy* that they lost?

Now don't get me wrong: I'm sure there are lots of pageant contestants who are able to move past the envy and be gracious nonwinners who are sincerely happy for the winner.

But my point is, even these women are likely not as happy as they appear to be. It's not that they aren't good people. It's just that, like all women, it's in our nature to want more for ourselves than we do for others.

Yes, we are flawed . . . totally and completely. We are all sinners with sin natures. As Paul points out, "All have sinned and fall short of the glory of God" (Rom. 3:23). But just in case you are tempted to stop there and blame everything on your fleshly condition, read on because the best part of this is yet to come. Being flawed is not the end of the story. It is not our pronounced sentence with no way out or no answer in sight . . . we are not victims to our nature. The most beautiful part of this equation is how that flaw gives us the ability to be better. For if there were no flaw, there would be no reason for forgiveness. And then we wouldn't get to see the awesome power of God miraculously at work in our lives.

WE ARE FORGIVEN COMPLETELY

The concept of God's forgiveness is beautiful yet mysterious. I don't know how well we ever really understand it, probably because genuine forgiveness by others so often eludes us on this earth. But at the same time, I believe God gives us lessons along the way that give us a glimpse into how very complete is His forgiveness of us as His children. For those of us who are parents, examples of this often center on our own children.

When my precious son Graham made a decision to accept Christ at the age of five, there were many things he did not yet know. He didn't know about God's sovereignty. He didn't know about God's power to heal the sick. He didn't know about the Trinity or all the ways of God. He didn't know all the reasons that accepting Christ at an early age would be the best and most important decision he would ever make. But one thing he clearly understood was God's forgiveness.

Graham had been interested in the things of God for several months, asking questions every now and then, but he had never shown that he wanted to make a salvation decision. On this particular night, Graham had exhibited some very bad behavior, and as a result, he was sent to his room and made to go to bed quite earlier than usual. After giving him a few minutes to think about what he had done, I was pleasantly surprised when I entered his room to tell him good night and saw a face that welcomed my presence, rather than one that scowled at me. *He must have done some hard thinking*, I thought. *Good.*

I knelt by Graham's bed and got as close to him as personal space would allow. With his head resting on his pillow, he looked at me with the big, beautiful eyes I loved so much and simply said, "Hi, Mom." I kissed his cheek and said, "Graham, you know I love you very much. I didn't want to have to send you to your room and make you miss out on playtime tonight. But I had to. Do you know why?" Graham answered quickly. "Yes. My attitude was really bad." "Yes, your attitude was bad, and so was your behavior," I said. "So the consequence of your choice is that you must go straight to bed without having any fun. I'm sorry, son. But this is the choice you made."

Graham's eyes revealed that he wanted to hear me say something more. I had a feeling I knew what that something was, so I continued. "Graham, I love you. And I forgive you for being disrespectful and having a bad attitude tonight. You are precious to me, and I'm not mad at you." Silent tears rolled down Graham's cheeks as he reached out for me. I reached out to him at the same time, and we embraced. He squeezed my neck as if he never wanted to let go. I sensed his gratitude toward me for loving him despite the things he had done that night.

While still intertwined in a hug, I began speaking to God in prayer. I thanked Him for Graham and for our many blessings and ended by thanking Him for the cross and what He had done to save us from our sins and forgive us for what we have done. After the amen, Graham was ready to talk. "Mommy?" he said. "Is a Christian someone who loves God?" "Yes," I answered. "A Christian not only loves God but also invites Him to live inside his heart and be his Lord and Savior." "Am I a Christian?" Graham asked. "Well, have you asked Jesus into your heart?" I asked. Graham thought for a minute and then asked the question every believing mother longs to hear her child say: "Can I pray right now?" "Of course!" I said, overjoyed. "Absolutely!"

> Jesus Christ loves and forgives you without conditions. Period.

At that moment, all my concerns about Graham being too young to understand and worrying about whether he fully grasped what he wanted to do went out the window. As I listened to my son purely ask Jesus to come into his heart, I realized Graham knew everything he needed to know at that moment. He knew Someone forgave him for the things he had done and loved him no matter what. He recognized through thinking about the cross that Jesus Christ demonstrated this love and forgiveness toward him. He had first seen it by me, his mom, in forgiving him and loving him despite his bad choices. But my five-year-old son knew that it went way beyond me and was really all about God. And he wanted to show Him he loved Him back by giving Him his heart.

Friend, you may not understand everything there is to know about the Bible. You may not have been raised in a Christian home, where Scripture was quoted daily and you were encouraged to have personal devotions. You may not have always lived a clean, godly life, and you may carry many scars from your past with you. But the one thing that even a five-year-old mind can grasp is the only thing you desperately need to know in your heart and in your soul: Jesus Christ loves and forgives you without conditions. Period.

But don't take my word for it. Just listen to what the psalmist says: "As far as the east is from the west, so far has he removed our transgressions from us" (Ps. 103:12). Transgressions are sins or wrongdoings we have done. And as a serial sinner, it is a very comforting thought for me to know that what Jesus did for me on the cross has separated me from my many sins.

But that is not the only beautiful aspect of this verse. The psalmist also paints for us a picture of the length to which God has gone to remove our sins: "as far as the east is from the west." So why did the psalmist illustrate the vastness of God's forgiveness with the distance of east to west, and not north from south? The reason is a very simple lesson in geography: because there is a measurable distance from the north to the south, but there is no measurable distance from the east to the west. God used those words because He wanted to illustrate for you and me that His forgiveness for us cannot be matched or measured! It is without conditions or limits. There is no cap on how many times He will forgive us.

Many verses in Scripture talk about God's forgiveness being undeserved and without merit. Daniel 9:9 says, "The Lord our God is merciful and forgiving, even though we have rebelled against him." Ephesians 1:7 says, "In him we have redemption through his blood, the forgiveness of sins, in accordance with the riches of God's grace." It is solely by the grace of God that we can be forgiven. And He is eager to do just that for each and every one of us. But in order to gain His forgiveness, we have to first realize that we need it. And that's where being flawed enters the picture.

> God used those words because He wanted to illustrate for you and me that His forgiveness for us cannot be matched or measured!

Luke 23 reminds us that there is no exception to this rule. In this chapter, we see that though deeply flawed, the criminal sentenced to die beside Jesus recognized his need to be forgiven and asked Jesus for this gift. The New Living Translation commentary describes it like this:

> As this man was about to die, he turned to Christ for forgiveness, and Christ accepted him. This shows that our deeds don't save us—our faith in Christ does. It is never too late to turn to God. Even in His misery, Jesus had mercy on this criminal who decided to believe in Him.[1]

We all need God's forgiveness, and He offers it to us, free of charge and expecting nothing in return. All we have to do is accept it. Jesus doesn't do with us what we often do with others by withholding forgiveness from them. He doesn't dangle His mercy over our head like a carrot only to pull it away when we reach for it. He lovingly and graciously extends it to us, despite our many flaws and failures in life.

While Satan would love for you to believe that you are too flawed and too unworthy of forgiveness, Jesus wants you to know that nothing could be farther from the truth.

There have been times in my life when looking in the mirror was hard for me because I knew who I was and what I had done. I sometimes felt as if I had a Kick Me sign on my back, and I was the first in line to do it. But when I realized in my heart and it began to sink into my soul that being so deeply flawed left me with the ability to be forgiven by God equally, the flaws suddenly felt really important to the process. And though I don't understand exactly how He is able to do that for me, I rejoice in its truth.

ten

THE TRUTH HEALS

You will know the truth, and the truth will set you free.

—John 8:32

Tell it to Jacob. You remember the story—Jacob is the guy in the Bible (Gen. 29) who discovered on his honeymoon that the woman he had just married after working seven years to have her was, in fact, her older sister, Leah. I mean, forget the fact that Leah wasn't as cute as the desired sister, Rachel. How about the fact that Jacob was deceived by his future father-in-law into marrying the wrong woman and had to work seven *more* years just to get the right one? Talk about a cruel joke! Jacob definitely found out the truth on his honeymoon, but did it set him free? Oddly enough, in some ways it probably did. At least now he had accurate information and could work toward his real goal of making Rachel his wife. But if you had asked Jacob moments after discovering the truth, I doubt if he would have described his feelings toward the situation as "set free." It was probably more like feeling "set up"!

Like Jacob, often when we find out who people really are, we tend to feel set up. This is especially true when it is a spiritual matter with a person claiming to be a spiritual guide or mentor or someone we have placed on a spiritual pedestal. We are shocked, if not angered, when they fall hundreds of feet off that pedestal after having their secret life of sin and depravity exposed for all the world to see. It makes us feel mad that they somehow pulled the wool over our eyes and caused us to believe they were something other than what they portrayed. Even if

> Often when we find out who people really are, we tend to feel set up.

the person wasn't actually trying to be someone she was not or trying to fool us into thinking she was different from what she actually was, we still feel resentful that the package we got is not measuring up to our perceived standard!

Michael English, a Christian recording artist who was once on top of the charts, is now possibly more famous (or infamous) for his extramarital affair with a fellow performer and musician in the mid-1990s. This man with an amazing talent and a beautiful voice is not the popular Christian artist he was on track to become. All his awards and accomplishments—after touring and performing for thousands and becoming a household name in Christian circles—all of it was severely overshadowed by this scandal.

Having real struggles is not exclusive to Michael English or anyone else. The truth is, in one way or another, we all show people the "us" we want them to see. Sometimes it is because we are insecure . . . or envious . . . or lonely. Many times we are afraid of rejection by others and don't think we can handle the way that would make us feel. But oftentimes it's because we don't understand who we are and who we were really meant to be, so we seek to be someone else . . . someone more exciting and engaging, perhaps . . . someone more talented or more together—a person who has a problem-free life.

Just like the scenario with the stylist in my hair salon . . . it was easier for me, at that moment, to pretend to Bree that I had it all together and didn't have a care in the world rather than admit to her that I sometimes really struggled with my weight, I wasn't a great wife sometimes, and my shopping has been known to get out of control. And besides the fact that this book was born that day in my heart, I learned something very important about myself at the salon: that although I pride myself on being genuine and real, the reality is that there is a very real limit to what I want people to actually know about me. And we are all that way.

Women, the truth *does* hurt: we are flawed . . . we are selfish . . . we are unlovely . . . and we are unworthy of the love of almighty God. But fortunately for us, that is not the end of the story. There is more truth we should know. The truth is also that we are loved . . . we are accepted . . . we are wanted . . . we are important to God . . . and we are His beautiful creations. With that knowledge, strangely enough, the truth of our total depravity now seems more like a gift than a curse. Together, these truths allow us to operate out of hearts of gratitude toward God and acceptance of ourselves so we can finally be the real us we were meant to be.

THE TRUTH, THE WHOLE TRUTH, AND NOTHING BUT THE TRUTH

For many years people have spent thousands of dollars visiting psychologists to try to figure out who they really are. While I am not a licensed psychologist, and I do not presume that I can help someone find herself in one book or one short chapter, I firmly believe that if one were to realize these three very basic truths based solidly on the Word of God, it could very well heal a life and might just stop the impersonations forever.

Truth #1: Recognition

God created you exactly the way you are, with your unique personality and temperament, since He is incapable of making a mistake.

God is infallible, meaning that He is flawless, is without error, and does not make mistakes. Deuteronomy 32:4 tells us, "He is the Rock, his works are perfect, and all his ways are just. A faithful God who does no wrong, upright and just is he." My godly parents taught me this beautiful truth as a child, and it is something, as an adult, I still strongly believe to be true.

But since I am human and have my own fallibilities and since I desire to be real with you in every area in this book, I have to admit to you that for years I was convinced God made a mistake when He created me. On the day He "knit me together in my mother's womb" (Ps. 139:13), I was sure that He was missing one of His knitting needles . . . I believed that He had performed a faux pas in creating me. I knew the correct Christian answer about how He made me exactly how

He wanted me to be and that He loved me just the way I am, but honestly, even at an early age I wondered how true that really was.

For years my struggle with identity centered on two things: my personality and my physical talents and abilities. As I shared in my previous book, *The 7 Hardest Things God Asks a Woman to Do*, I have the most precious and godly of all mothers. She is kind and selfless, and everyone who meets her falls in love with her. She is the kind of woman everyone wants to get close to because she makes them feel important. God has blessed my mother with a special spirit,

> God is infallible, meaning that He is flawless, is without error, and does not make mistakes.

and it is no secret to anyone around her. I always wanted to be just like her, and it was difficult to do that when my DNA structure was so different from hers. I would constantly try to adjust myself to act like her, talk like her, and be like her, but it never worked.

I was always too controversial. I had strong opinions and ideas that didn't easily remain hidden. I was strong, assertive, and bold. I had a mouth that would hinge open anytime I felt an injustice was done, and try as I did, I could not get that hinge to stay shut. Trying to morph myself into the sweet, submissive, often quiet, carefree spirit of my mom never worked well and led me to become frustrated and disappointed in what I thought God should have changed when He created me.

But it wasn't just my personality that I had a problem with. I was also convinced that God really messed up the talent portion of me as well. Like many young girls, I admired and adored popular singers such as Debbie Boone, Amy Grant, The

Cruse Family, The Second Chapter of Acts, and Evie. On any given day you could find me in one of my mother's full slips (think evening gown) with a hairbrush or curling iron in my hand being used as a microphone. Long before karaoke was cool, I was performing my own songs from my playroom stage in front of an audience of stuffed animals! I would sing my heart out as the record played. I would pretend I was the real artist onstage, ministering to thousands with my angelic voice. I absolutely loved music and wanted to be a singer someday.

Though my record player is long gone and I no longer have time for pretend performances on a makeshift stage, I still get the same feelings I had as a little girl when my favorite music is played. While my musical repertoire has changed, and I now prefer Caedmon's Call and Alicia Keys to KC and the Sunshine Band and Shaun Cassidy, the emotions are the same. I now understand that the emotions I have when I hear music are spiritual in nature as God ministers to me through music in a way I sometimes can't even comprehend. Music moves me and motivates me. It gets me in the mindset to worship, and I am so grateful for the gift of music in my life. I couldn't love music more. But having said that, let me also say this: I can love music all I want, but that doesn't mean that I was created to be a musician.

The truth is I can't sing all that well. (Ouch . . . I said it!) I might be good enough to blend with an ensemble, but I am not solo artist material. I don't have the range other musicians have, and I sing from my throat instead of my diaphragm. Oh, and one more thing . . . I have extreme anxiety and stage fright about singing in front of an audience. For some reason, that tends to hinder the possibilities of singing onstage just a tad!

But ask me to speak onstage, and I have no problem whatsoever. I have always been able to speak to large groups of people from the stage with only mild nervousness. Hmm . . . is that an irony? A coincidence? Or perhaps, a divine calling instead of a manufactured dream? I could spend my time and life pining away for something to change and to be the singer I have always wanted to be, but why? Is it healthy? Is it productive? Is it even possible?! No.

I can get proper vocal training and find ways to handle my anxiety over singing onstage, but I have the feeling that won't do the trick. I can duct-tape my mouth shut and stand in a corner, but that won't work in the long run. I will still be a square peg trying to fit into a round hole when it comes to what God created me to do and who He created me to be. One day, when I go to be with God and my earthly limitations are no more, I will be able to sing with the angels and sound just like one of them. But for right now, my calling is not that of a singer or an introvert with a passive personality. I know it . . . and I now accept it.

I never tire of reading the psalm about my creation because it reminds me of the deliberateness of God's craftsmanship of me. "You made all the delicate, inner parts of my body and knit me together in my mother's womb. Thank you for making me so wonderfully complex! Your workmanship is marvelous—how well I know it" (139:13–14 NLT).

It is important not only to read this verse but also to personalize it for yourself. The genius master inventor, Jesus Christ, came up with the concept of you . . . and me . . . and everyone else in the entire universe, starting with Adam in the garden! Phenomenal!

It has been a beautiful thing in my life to let go of the ideas

I have for me and ask God to develop in me those things He intends me to do and to be the person He intends me to be. Please don't misunderstand me—it's not wrong to have a love for something or a desire for something, and I firmly believe women should have goals and dreams and aspirations. I believe we should reach higher to achieve things and have great determination to fulfill standards we set for ourselves . . . that is not what I am talking about. I am talking about saying to God, "Have Your own way with me." Recognize that in the process of making you, God didn't have an "oops!" moment. He didn't make a mistake in creating the person you are because He is incapable of such a thing. Any mistakes that were made along the way (when we were old enough to make them ourselves) were made by us. Which brings me to the next very important truth.

Truth #2: Admission

God created you with a free will to choose your behavior and mess up your life.

My husband is a man of many sayings. So many sayings, in fact, that his friends and I sometimes call them *Scottyisms*. Some of them are funny . . . some of them are corny . . . and some of them blow me away with their wisdom. One of my favorite Scottyisms is something he says to our children a lot. Being ten, seven, and five, their young world revolves around how much fun they can have on a daily basis and how to avoid breaking rules in the process of trying to have fun!

Inevitably, one of our children will break a rule and will have to face the music by losing a privilege. When this happens, human nature usually sets in, and they complain with great intensity about how completely unfair it all is. Scotty will then look at them and say, "Guys, I want you to have fun. Daddy will never take away your fun. The only one who can take away your fun is *you*." It's a classic Scottyism, and it is also a great lesson about how God relates to us, His children.

Make no mistake about it, God desires for us to have beautiful and fulfilling lives. He doesn't want us to endure all the heartache that accompanies bad choices, wrong decisions, and distorted life views. But He is also just and righteous, and He often allows our mistakes to guide us into better choices for our futures.

In Nehemiah 9, after leading the once-exiled Israelites to rebuild the crumbling walls of Jerusalem, Nehemiah faced the problem of dealing with a sinful bunch of people. Wisely recognizing that he was more of an administrator than a preacher, he turned the job of repairing the people's hearts over to Ezra, the priest. As Ezra read God's law to them, the Israelites were inspired to confess their sins and to change their evil ways. Yet their flesh continued to draw them back to a place of sin and depravity.

In the ninth chapter of Nehemiah, Ezra implores them to take a good, hard look at their lives and reminds them of the mercy of God, despite all of their past sins:

> But when all was going well, your people turned to sin again, and once more you let their enemies conquer them. Yet whenever your people returned to you and cried to you for help, once more you listened from heaven, and in your wonderful mercy delivered them! You punished them in order to turn them toward your laws; but even though they should have obeyed them, they were proud and wouldn't listen, and continued to sin. You were patient with them for

many years. You sent your prophets to warn them about their sins, but still they wouldn't listen. So once again you allowed the heathen nations to conquer them. But in your great mercy you did not destroy them completely or abandon them forever. What a gracious and merciful God you are! (vv. 28–31 TLB)

Just as God dealt with the sinful Israelites, so He deals with our sinful society. As parents do not desire to see their children hurt and unhappy, God is truly merciful and does not desire to see His children hurt by the consequences of their actions. But while He doesn't desire for us to endure this, He will often allow the natural progression of consequences to occur for us as sometimes it is the one and only way for us to "get" that we have, in fact, caused our own pain and messed up our own lives.

It may sound a bit harsh at first to say that we mess it up . . . I know. But it is an important truth to recognize and admit. It's not about being stuck in a quicksand of regret although that is something Satan would like for us to do. Taking responsibility for our choices is something we simply must do in order to be able to own them, to forgive ourselves for them (and ask God to forgive us of them), and to move on to a place where our authenticity with others is no longer blocked because of our self-imposed stigma.

> God desires for us to have beautiful and fulfilling lives . . . But He often allows our mistakes to guide us into better choices for our futures.

One of the things I find interesting about this truth deals with the fact that we, women especially, seem to be always fighting for our rights . . . to be free, to be able to make decisions for ourselves and to be independent and respected. But then when we make choices in the name of independence, we don't like to own our decisions and see them for what they are—choices that carry consequences. When the mess-ups come, we want to pass the buck or play the blame game with a parent, a spouse, a boyfriend, a friend, our church, and even our children. It's as if it is too painful to admit that we have caused much of our own pain in our lives, and we continue to do so.

Rest assured that the mess-ups will happen for all of us. Remember, it's in our nature, and no one is perfect except for God. But that is not an excuse for our behavior. In addition to our nature, we each have been given a free will, which is a beautiful thing when exercised in a healthy and God-centered way. It's when we make choices that lead us down self-destructive paths that we suffer, not because we are being punished by an ogre of a God who wants to see us live unhappily ever after.

But in the process of admitting our mess-ups, we are not to get down on ourselves and continually beat up ourselves for it. Satan would love for us to do that so we can then be stifled in our usefulness for God and prompted to try to fake out everyone by being a different person. But rather, we should use our mistakes as reminders of what life is like without God's guidance and determine to reject going down those paths again.

> Rest assured that the mess-ups will happen for all of us.

Unfortunately, the way we deal with our mistakes is much like a frustrated dieter often deals with falling off the diet wagon. The once-dedicated calorie counter has for weeks carefully monitored what she has put into her body. Then, suddenly, she blows it one day, consuming large amounts of fatty food and way too many carbs. Disgusted with herself, she decides to then just continue her eating binge, resulting in more weight gain and further self-loathing. Instead of stopping at one mistake (in the form of a chocolate-glazed doughnut), she has proceeded to make several others, thereby putting on more weight than she ever would have if she would've stopped with the first one!

All of us have been guilty of this kind of behavior at one time or another. And all of us have caused ourselves pain that could have been avoided if we had sought God's counsel and not believed Satan's lie. But God is quick not only to forgive us; He is quick also to restore us.

There are many biblical examples of people who messed up and were greatly used for God's glory. In fact, I think God likely included so many mess-ups in the Bible because He knew how often we would mess up and that we would need many points of reference to encourage us to move on! Until his conversion, the apostle Paul (once known as Saul) used to track down and hurt Christians (Acts 8–9). Martha missed the mark and made mistakes (Luke 10:38–42). Thomas doubted God (John 20:25). Peter betrayed his Lord (Matt. 26:69–75). David, a man after God's own heart, fouled up in a big way when he lusted, had an affair, and took part in a murder plot (2 Sam. 11). All of these mess-ups share the same commonality that you and I do: that of a divine and holy God bringing colossal failures back to His fold and restoring them once again.

> God is quick not only to forgive us; He is quick also to restore us.

I am reminded daily that God often uses broken people—the people with the most baggage—for His honor and glory. As I write this book, please know that I am nowhere near baggage-free. I am a self-proclaimed "mess-up" whom God has graciously chosen to forgive and use for His glory. Do I deserve it? No way. But I am eager to embrace it.

But though He restores us, God does not leave us wondering how we are to live our lives. In Scripture, we are exhorted over and over to conduct ourselves purely and to make right choices with the free will we have been given. Paul reminds us about this in Ephesians:

> So be careful how you live. Don't live like fools, but like those who are wise. Make the most of every opportunity in these evil days. Don't act thoughtlessly, but understand what the Lord wants you to do. Don't be drunk with wine, because that will ruin your life. Instead, be filled with the Holy Spirit, singing psalms and hymns and spiritual songs among yourselves, and making music to the Lord in your hearts. (5:15–19 NLT)

God wants us to understand that it is in our best interest to follow Him and live according to His truth instead of the "truth" offered up by the world. He doesn't want us to mess up our lives by the choices we make that will eventually destroy us.

Before I move on to the next truth, please allow me to address something that many of you are likely dealing with. Some of us have been victims of someone else's bad choices that have caused major hurts and mess-ups in our lives. I know that. Please know that if you are a victim of molestation, rape, incest, or any other violation of your body and soul, God does not hold you responsible for those things, and neither should you. Those things are unequivocally not your fault, and you are not to be stigmatized by them or defined by them or ruled by them. Psalm 10:14 is a precious reminder of how God feels about those who have been victimized by others: "You, O God, do see trouble and grief; you consider it to take it in hand. The victim commits himself to you; you are the helper of the fatherless."

The beautiful thing about life with Jesus Christ is that He understands your pain and looks upon you with mercy and love and deep empathy and grace. He does not judge you or hold you responsible for the actions of others when you were unable to make a choice for yourself. So please know that this truth is not about a victim being held responsible for a decision she did not herself make. And even if you have been the victimizer of someone else, you can move past that. You can make things well with your soul by amending those bad decisions with the one you harmed and with God. None of us is exempt from causing our own mess-ups. Whether you were a victim or a victimizer, contrary to what Satan would have you believe, one bad choice or consequence does not have to lead to another . . . and another . . . and another.

> I am reminded daily that God often uses broken people— the people with the most baggage—for His honor and glory.

We all make bad choices in life. Maybe it's sexual. Maybe it's in choosing a life partner or inside the marriage where we mess up. Maybe it's about what to ingest into our bodies and our minds, choices that are toxic to our system and can be cleansed only with the help of Jesus Christ. But it's not about the bad choices we have made or living with the guilt hanging over our heads. Remember, we are completely flawed yet forgiven completely. The truth is that in order to be genuine . . . authentic . . . real . . . and without pretense, we have to own our mistakes and not allow them to rule over us but to motivate us from this point forward to seek God first in our lives.

Truth #3: Resolution

God created us to discern and discover who we are and where we function most effectively, without trying to be someone else.

Discovering who we are is the very important first step. Owning up to our mistakes in the past is the next integral part of the process. Resolving to just be you and no one else is the last component, and it will ultimately determine the fate of your role-playing in the future.

I recently had an experience that illustrated this truth for me. I did not go looking to find it, and I certainly didn't expect to find it in a fast-food restaurant. But that is exactly where it happened.

I had just attended my weekly aerobics class and was feeling pretty hungry. Nearing my house, I decided to pull into the strip mall a mile away and grab a sandwich from Subway, the chain famous for its delicious made-to-order sandwiches. I was sweaty and hot, but I couldn't wait to sink my teeth into the sandwich of my choice: turkey on wheat with mustard and vinegar and all the veggies (hold the black olives and jalapenos) two pieces of bread can handle. Entering the store, I realized that this fast-food stop was going to be anything but fast because the store was packed with hungry consumers.

I fell in line behind four others, dutifully waiting my turn as I watched the sandwich artists go to work fielding requests and creating masterpieces out of lunch meat and lettuce. One by one the customers called out their preferences: a meatball with extra cheese on Italian bread with onions and black olives . . . a roast beef and ham on white bread with spinach, tomatoes, sweet sauce, oil and vinegar, jalapenos, and cucumbers . . . a teriyaki chicken on toasted sun-dried tomato bread with nothing but lettuce and salt and pepper . . . and a veggie on wheat with extra pickles and green peppers, hold the cheese, mayo, and mustard. With each order, I nearly gagged . . . wondering how someone could eat such a horrible sandwich. I couldn't believe some of the combinations these people were ordering. I didn't understand why in the world they wouldn't want something like a turkey on wheat with mustard and vinegar and all the veggies two pieces of bread could handle. Now *that* was a good sandwich!

> Resolving to just be you and no one else . . . will ultimately determine the fate of your role-playing in the future.

As I waited for my turn to order, a thought occurred to me. Although I did not prefer a meatball sub, a teriyaki chicken, a roast beef and ham, or a veggie hold the cheese, the people in line in front of me ordering them *did*. And their taste buds were as excited as mine were about delving into the sandwich of their choice as soon as they paid for it. And they likely weren't attracted to my turkey on wheat either. Standing in line, I was impressed with the fact that although we were all in the same place and ordering a certain type of food, we were all going about it in a very different way. We were a diverse group in that Subway that day, likely in more ways than just our preference of hoagies.

This very simple illustration shows how individual we are, even down to our taste buds. We are unique and different, and that is beautiful. We aren't like the subdivisions so popular now where the houses are cookie-cutter images of each other, having varying outsides but all looking the same on the inside! You can dress yourself up to look like the "house" next to you, but that will not make you more like her. And the truth is you wouldn't want to be even though you might think so. Make no mistake about it: we all have downsides to our personalities. Even when we see someone we identify with perfection . . . it's a mirage! She is not perfect, and she struggles with things . . . maybe not the same things you or I do, but she struggles too. And as we begin to look at people that way, we will become less and less intimidated by them. We will learn to care less about what they think of us and more about what God thinks of us. Certainly not in a callous way, but in the proper perspective of who we are in the eyes of God.

We need to praise God for the downsides to our personalities and gloriously embrace them because it is not really a self-esteem issue but a spiritual one. For were He to have made us without downsides and weak areas of our personalities, we would have no need for Him in our lives! We would be adequate without His help—not the way He intended it to be. When I look at it this way, I am reminded of God's complete sovereignty. He was a genius in crafting you and me, and He didn't omit any detail or leave anything to chance. And I believe that it's time for us to stop wasting our time trying to be the girl to our right instead of being the best *me* all of us can be for the glory of God. He deserves it, and we owe it to Him. "Therefore, I urge you, brothers, in view of God's mercy, to offer your bodies as living sacrifices, holy and pleasing to God—this is your spiritual act of worship" (Rom. 12:1).

In this era of sexual promiscuity and free sexual expression, I have noticed something that makes me appreciate God even more. As I have surrendered to Him in a greater way and have worked on myself through prayer and seeking God and godly counsel, God has begun to use me in a way I didn't think possible. And in an ironic way, it leads me back to this point. Hang in there with me . . . I promise to explain what I mean in a minute.

> I am reminded of God's complete sovereignty. He was a genius in crafting you and me, and He didn't omit any detail or leave anything to chance.

One night I was speaking to a group of women, and after I finished speaking I walked off the stage and just kept walking. I didn't know where I was going, and moments later I finally stopped and found myself in another part of the building. After pouring my heart out in my message, I was both mentally and physically exhausted. I sat down in a chair and exhaled. I felt like a balloon that had just let out its air with feelings of sheer and utter emptiness. But not in the way you might think.

I felt empty of me. But I felt so full of God I could hardly breathe. And on a completely different level than I had ever experienced before, I realized what it felt like to truly be used by God. I thought about the irony in the fact that I had allowed someone to take me over and use me—and it didn't feel gross or inappropriate or draining or sinful. In truth, it was the only time in my life I can remember that being "used" by someone felt good.

That, my dear friend, is the beauty and irony of allowing God to use you with your gifts and talents and personality for His glory. I can assure that if you resolve to discern and determine who God created you to be and where you function best, He will do His part and use you as His servant. When we resolve to be the person we should be and allow ourselves to be used by God, a sweet coupling happens that changes us forever. And it feels fantastic.

A SOOTHING BALM VERSUS A HEALING BALM

There is a balm in Gilead,
to make the wounded whole,
there is a balm in Gilead,
to heal the sin sick soul.

Sometimes I feel discouraged,
and think my work's in vain,
but then the Holy Spirit
revives my soul again.

If you cannot preach like Peter,
if you cannot pray like Paul,
You can tell the love of Jesus,
and say He died for all.[1]

I remember hearing this spiritual, "There Is a Balm in Gilead," as a young girl and thinking its words sounded funny. A bomb in Gilead? What in the world is that? Where is Gilead? And why would someone want to bomb it? It took several years for me to realize that I had the pronunciation wrong . . . it was a *balm*, not a *bomb*, and Gilead was a place we would likely never go on any of our family vacations. But while my young mind had a hard time processing such things back then, now I get it. A balm is like modern-day aloe vera, which we put on bad sunburns after an extended day out at the beach. A balm soothes. A balm comforts. A balm relieves.

This balm in Gilead is referred to in several places in Scripture, one of which is Jeremiah 46:11. Here the Lord says (through His messenger Jeremiah) to the sinful Egyptian people, "Go up to Gilead and get balm . . . You multiply remedies in vain." His reference to this balm in Gilead was a reminder to them that a quick cure would not fix their problems in the long term.

A soothing balm can only do so much. While it is welcome relief to the well-cooked sunbather and while it can provide some temporary relief to other abrasions and skin irritations we may encounter from time to time, it cannot completely heal the really deep wounds. A balm has topical benefits only, so it doesn't go beyond the surface in order to heal from the inside out.

But a healing balm . . . now, that is quite different. To heal something is to provide a long-term cure for, to mend, to make well, and to repair. And when it comes to our souls, there is no topical ointment that will help. There is no amount of anesthetizing that we can do—no topical things that temporarily make us feel better, such as sex, alcohol, drugs, and religions. Those may momentarily feel good but will never give lasting relief because they are not the right remedy for a hurting heart. Often we continue to pile them on, hoping one day they will miraculously and suddenly work for us, yet they never do.

Because of our free will, God says to us today as He said to the people of Egypt by way of Jeremiah, "Go on ahead, girl, and try those things if you want to. I wish you wouldn't, but I gave you a free will to make your own choices in life. You can try them . . . but they won't work. And I'll be waiting for you when you find out that they don't" (my paraphrase).

Know this, my sisters and friends: Jesus is the only One who can truly heal our souls, from the inside out. The healing balm He provides is on a different level altogether from any other soothing balm. The results of His balm in our lives are not temporary and don't wipe off, wear off, or come off. It's not a quick fix. The balm of our heavenly Father is the gift of peace and joy and spiritual growth and unconditional love that is ours for the taking. And it is the gift that allows us to know the sometimes-ugly truth about ourselves, and yet be set free by it.

Time is a perfect example of a soothing balm. There is an old debate that still rages, and that is the debate on whether "time heals all wounds." Some people believe it, and some people don't. Lots of people say it, but is it true? Certainly, time has a way of softening hard feelings, fuzzying the facts, and creating distance between the present from the past. Time is a tool God gives us to help grow us, mature us, and mercifully allow us to finally get a place of recognition and maturity that it is ultimately all about Him in the first place. And time can be a soothing balm, like a topical ointment that helps a stinging soul feel a bit better.

But it is my belief that while time is often helpful to us, time in and of itself does not *heal* anything. Ask a person whose loved one died unexpectedly. Talk to a mother whose child died before his time. I have heard the loved ones left behind testify to the fact that no matter how many years it has been, time never totally takes away the pain that comes with their loss. It may help ease the pain a bit, but it doesn't heal it. To say that it does takes away from the one and only thing that truly heals: *Jesus Christ.*

Truth is God. God is Truth. The truth only heals because God is Truth. "I am the way, the truth, and the life" (John 14:6 NKJV). An incredible thing happens when the Truth is known. The Truth (Jesus Christ) is the only thing that holds the power to totally set a soul free. There's only one Truth—the healing balm of Jesus—that can do something so powerful and miraculous and . . . amazing.

> Know this, my sisters and friends: Jesus is the only One who can truly heal our souls, from the inside out.

IMPERSONATIONS, NO MORE

Popular comedian and actor Eddie Murphy took home a Golden Globe award in 2007 for his performance in the movie *Dreamgirls.* After going through an acrimonious divorce in 2006, in his acceptance speech, Eddie thanked his new girlfriend of a few months for "fixing everything that was broken." As I watched the footage of the awards show and heard him say this, I was struck by the statement, and it has been on my mind ever since. Here are a few of my personal reflections about this statement:

I have a precious husband who supports me, loves me, and is amazingly connected to my needs. But still . . . he has never fixed everything in me that was broken.

I have three beautiful children who are a fulfillment of a life dream of becoming a mother. They adore me, encourage me, and enrich every day of my life, but they have never been able to fix everything in me that was broken.

I have wonderful parents who raised me to love God and have a deep and personal faith in Him, despite life's difficulties. They are always in my corner and are my cheerleaders in life. But they haven't been able to fix everything that has been broken.

I have a best girlfriend whom I couldn't be fonder of, with whom I can be totally real, and who knows me inside and out and still thinks I'm the most special friend she has ever had. I get lots of things from her, but she hasn't ever been able to fix my broken places.

I have a circle of friends and family, including my church family, who provide me with true community and love. They are an amazing team of brothers and sisters whom I deeply love, but they have not been able to fix anything that was broken.

He desires to take our broken places and set us free by the Truth that we were once so afraid to face.

I've tried things over the years that are considered helpful by the world's standards in forgetting any problems I might have. But any momentary pleasure of this world that I have ever partaken of has never fixed anything in my life that was broken and always made the problems—and me—more broken.

I've read many inspirational books and quotes and articles in my life. But any self-help book or advice I have read—while sometimes making me feel good with its positive principles for life or helping me have a more positive outlook on that day—has never fixed anything in my life that was broken.

I've reached goals in my life that may be considered successful by some. But any accomplishment I have ever had or accolade I have ever received has never done anything to fix my broken parts, no matter how sweet success felt at the time.

I readily admit that I've never been raped, beaten, or arrested. But rest assured, I have had other significant broken places in my life that needed to be fixed. Broken places over relationships, bad choices, mistakes, indulgences, inadequacies, serious hurts, physical pain . . . broken by me and sometimes by others. But in all my brokenness, the only cure I have ever found that works is the one found in Jesus Christ. And it's not because He's one more thing to try—it's because He is the I AM, the Truth that heals, and there is no other. And He desires to take our broken places and set us free by the Truth that we were once so afraid to face.

Some years ago, my brother, Mark, gave me a book as a birthday gift. It is a compilation of one woman's conversations with God as she struggled to find her heavenly Father in the midst of her personal suffering. I have referred to it many times over the years when dealing with my own trials, and its words are beautiful and raw and real. I want to share with you an especially meaningful piece to me entitled "My God, Do You Love Me—Truly Love Me?"

When I doubt that you hear my cries
When I feel I am one of billions of humans
Inhabiting this planet
It's hard to feel special to you.
Do you frown at such times, or do you hear my longing
    to know
I have a loving, responsive Father?
Are you aware of my struggle

To feel I have worth in your eyes,
Especially when I knowingly sin
Or fail to live up to my own expectations?
Ah, Father—Are you privy to the childhood pain,
To the memories I haven't been able to exorcise?
Do you witness my attempts to connect emotionally
With my husband, children, close friends—
Attempts that sometimes falter?
What do you think of my drivenness—
My breathless attempts to impress others
With my accomplishments and good deeds?
And do you judge me as harshly as I judge myself,
Or do you carry me and my concerns
In some small corner of your vast heart
Tenderly watching over me
As a mother watches over her child?
I need to know where we stand, Lord.
I need to feel I am not alone.
I need to know that you care, that you love me
With an intense, enduring love
That will carry me softly into eternity.
My God, do you love even me?[2]

Jesus does not skip a beat when He is asked this question. There is no awkward pause in His response. In case you're wondering, here's His answer back to you . . .

- ✦ *I love you so much that I took the time to create you.* (Gen. 1:27)
- ✦ *I love you so much that I desire to stay constantly connected to you.* (1 Cor. 1:9)

❖ *I love you so much that I know everything about you, even the number of hairs on your head.* (Matt. 10:30; Luke 12:7)

❖ *I love you so much that I forgave you for everything you have ever done.* (Ps. 65:3)

❖ *I love you so much that I died on the cross to save you.* (John 3:16–17)

❖ *I love you so much that I am coming again to take you to a perfect place to live with Me forever.* (John 14:1–3)

The gentleman that He is, Jesus is simply waiting for you to decide to take His hand and let Him lead you down a path of life and truth. He offers to you and to me a life more beautiful and fulfilling than we could ever hope for or imagine. It's ours for the taking, if we will let go of the facades and just be real. As George Washington Carver once said, "Our creator is the same and never changes despite the names given Him by people here and in all parts of the world. Even if we gave Him no name at all, He would still be there, within us, waiting to give us good on this earth."

Jesus is waiting for you right this very minute. And He wants to set you free.

DESPERATELY SEEKING YOU

In chapter 1, I told you about a movie called *Desperately Seeking Susan*. The name of the movie comes from the newspaper ad placed by someone to find a woman named Susan. But as I think about this movie and its title, I can't help but wonder if Jesus placed a personal ad for you, what might it say? I think it would say something like this:

Desperately seeking you, the one I love. No shade or color. No size, shape, or status. No stigmas attached, and no hesitations. No restrictions or boundaries. No red flags, pretenses, or conditions. No facades allowed. No charades accepted. Love without boundaries. Acceptance without limits. The love of your life and the craving of your soul. Someone to fix all of your broken places.

Desperately seeking *you*.

Jesus is searching for you, but are you looking for Him? You may not know it yet, but you are. You might be turning to a quick fix or temporary solution, a few pills, a night out on the town, or a religion full of empty promises. You might be longing for a place to fit in or someone to call family. In the deepest part of your heart, you may be pleading for someone to be there for you, someone who won't hurt you or ever let you down. You are looking for Jesus Christ and the Truth only He can offer you.

Jesus desperately wants for us to know He loves and accepts us . . . fully . . . completely . . . totally . . . from top to bottom and tip to toe, when no one else does . . . without the facades, without the pretense, and without all the fluff. He wants us to realize the freedom—true freedom—that comes with letting go of the struggle, once and for all, over our past mistakes, major life interruptions, and wrongs that have been done to us. He desires to remove that which has incapacitated us and held us captive—unable to fly and soar and be the beautifully created person He has made us each to be. Jesus wants to fix everything in us that has ever been broken, not temporarily soothing it on the exterior, but healing it in places not able to be seen by the human eye. He has always been around . . . just waiting on us to finally understand what this life thing is really all about.

THE TRUTH THAT SETS US FREE

I had a dream once, several years ago. It made absolutely no sense at the time I dreamed it, but it was one of those dreams that you remember in the morning and think about throughout the day and, possibly, the rest of your life.

It was a beautiful dream, with an ethereal background of white billows and breezy air. But it was not a dream about heaven. In the dream, all I could see were puzzle pieces. They were of no particular picture, but they were shifting around . . . first one way and then another. They were moving—floating—in midair, appearing to be looking for their places, trying to find their perfect fit. There were no words, and no hands were visibly seen to be guiding the puzzle pieces as they searched for their home within the puzzle. Then suddenly, one by one, they clicked into place, first one and then another. And although the picture was not a visual in my mind, the puzzle pieces very distinctively came together to form a whole and complete puzzle.

My dear girlfriend, you may not see the hands of God guiding you through your life or bringing pieces of your "puzzle" together. But His care for you can be found, if you will choose to see it . . . by the way He knit you together in your mother's womb, laid down His life for you in a selfless act of unconditional love, and searches for you as if you are the only one He is interested in finding. His arms are a place of ultimate security and peaceful rest. You may not be able to physically see Him in this lifetime, but rest assured, He is the most real person you will ever know.

Embrace your heritage. Accept who you are, and find out who God created you to be. Free yourself from the comparisons and impersonations of others. Then and only then you will finally be able to become the whole and authentically real woman who trusts and values and believes and hopes.

Accept the truths found in God's Word about who you are: *completely flawed yet forgiven completely; an awesome spirit being, truly loved and accepted by God.* Though these concepts seem way too good to be true . . . they are true. And when we fully realize them in our lives, any attempts to impersonate perfection, confidence, happiness, or spirituality would be completely out of the question.

Discovering the truth about who we are takes away our need to be anyone else. And that, my friend, is the Truth that will, once and for all, set your soul free.

BIBLE STUDY GUIDE

My dear girlfriends,

Thank you for letting me share my heart with you in the ten chapters of this book. The message in *Behind Those Eyes* is a simple yet crucial one: *we need to get real*—real with one another . . . real with ourselves . . . and real before God. Sure, we can stay pretenders for as long as we choose. But it won't get us any closer to becoming the women we desperately desire to be. And aren't we tired of pretending anyway?

This Bible study guide, divided by the book chapters, has several sections: *Reality Check* (what I most want you to take away from the chapter), *Challenge Verse* (a short scripture for you to meditate on and/or memorize), *Truth Talk* (questions for group discussion and/or personal reflection), *Behind Your Eyes* (where I cut to the chase and help you probe deep into your soul for answers), *Challenge Question* (a thought-provoking challenge question), and *Getting Real* (a specific call to action to help you live out what you have learned). These sections are meant to help you process the information and facilitate further personal study of God's Word.

My greatest desire is that through this book and this study, you will be inspired to choose authenticity over pretense and impersonation. I pray that the questions will bring forth genuine soul searching, resulting in a radical transformation toward truthfulness in your own life. Will you join me today on the truth-seeking journey? Ready to get real?

Be encouraged . . . be prayerful . . . and be *you*!

Lisa

P. S.

To the Bible study leaders . . . thank you for being willing to facilitate truth talk by leading out in this study. Though I recognize that some of the questions (particularly in the *Behind Your Eyes* section) may not be completely comfortable at first for your group to discuss, I am praying that truthful dialogue will occur among you. It is my heartfelt belief that transparency with others is an important part in our process of authenticity. I am confident that you will approach each subject with genuine care and discernment as you lead women to uncover what is truly behind their eyes. May God give you the grace to be a transparent leader. Dig deep!

one THE TRUTH HURTS

Reality Check

Sitting in my hair appointment the day I met Bree, the stylist I introduced to you in the first chapter, I had this book stirring in my heart. I knew that if I were feeling a heartfelt desire to get real, you, my girlfriends, were feeling it too. I won't lie to you. The truth does sometimes hurt. There may be a small cost to authenticity. Maybe it will be a bit uncomfortable or unfamiliar to some of us to finally get real. Perhaps it won't always please people to hear or tell the truth. But it is my belief that there is a much bigger price tag for continuing to live a life of pretense and impersonation. This chapter explains why we pretend, how we pretend, and why our souls crave much more.

Challenge Verse

What you're after is truth from the inside out.
—Psalm 51:6 MSG

Truth Talk

1. Define the word *authenticity* and what it means to you. How can you tell if someone is being genuine and real, or can you tell?

2. Jesus often called people to get real through His appointed messengers (such as Paul in his writings to the New Testament churches). What do you think His message is to us today? Is it the same or different? How?

3. Read 1 Peter 1:7. Notice that Peter is talking about facing trials in order to prove genuine faith. Spiritually speaking, what does it mean to be truthful, genuine, and real? Do you see why difficulties can bring out the truth though the process may be hurtful?

4. Is there a correlation between spiritual truth and earthly truth? How could your lack of spiritual pretense help you in your relationships with others on this earth?

5. Think about this statement: cover-ups meet a need to get us more of what we want at the time when we don't think the truth will. Besides Judas, think of some other biblical examples of people who did this. One very familiar incident happened just prior to the crucifixion and involved a betrayal of Jesus in order to escape personal ridicule and ramifications due to association (Matt. 26; Mark 14). Who was involved and what happened? Why didn't he choose truth at that moment?

6. Think of a relationship you have that you consider to be based on truth—one that is authentic and real. Who is it with? What makes it real? Now think of a relationship that isn't. What's the difference?

Behind Your Eyes

1. Your challenge verse and the verse at the beginning of chapter 1 is Psalm 51:6: "What you're after is truth from the inside out." Is this true in your life? Do you recognize the

need in this world for greater authenticity? What about in your relationships? Why?

2. Can you recall a time in your life when the truth hurt you and caused you to react negatively? Positively?

3. Recall a time when you felt it was in your best interest to keep the truth hidden. What made you feel that way? Was it helpful or hurtful in the end?

4. In chapter 1, I recall a time when, as a young girl, I pretended to be a pageant queen on the trunk of my dad's car and was embarrassed when I was discovered doing it. Can you think of a time when you knew pretending wasn't a good idea?

Challenge Question

Be honest . . . what is your deepest soul craving? What have you tried to do to satisfy it, both negatively and/or positively?

Getting Real

Pray today that God will reveal one important truth to you about yourself, regardless of how painful it is to hear. Commit to praying for that in your life if change needs to occur.

Oh, Jesus. Help us to get real.
Help us to see that pretending was not
in Your original plan for our lives.
Convince us by Your Holy Spirit that authenticity
and genuineness are important enough to come
out of hiding. Clean out the corners of our hearts
that we try to keep secret from You and everyone else.
In Jesus' name. Amen.

two MS. PERFECTION

Reality Check

When I think of Ms. Perfection, I feel so tired. After all, it is hard to keep up the pace of acting perfect. Yet for so much effort, many of us can see ourselves in this role. It is the role most often impersonated by women, largely due to the fact that we want others to view us through a flawless lens. Within our desire to be seen as put together and perfect, we find the roles of perfect wife, perfect mom, and perfect package. This chapter dispels the myth that perfection is possible, regardless of which role Ms. Perfection seeks to play.

Challenge Verse

Even perfection has its limits, but your commands have no limit. —Psalm 119:96 NLT

Truth Talk

1. If you are with a group, discuss the "Great Sunday Morning Fakeout." (If you're by yourself, think about it.) Is this type of situation widespread? What facilitates it?

2. What do you feel makes us want people to see us as perfect? Why does it matter so much?

3. Why is it important to recognize that perfection is not humanly possible?

4. Can you think of a woman in Scripture who suffered from this perfection syndrome? Consider the story of Martha. Read Luke 10:38–42 and write down your thoughts about it. Is Martha's attitude harmless? Why or why not?

5. Did you see the symbolism of the pen mark on my skirt while in church in relation to striving for perfection? Have you ever had a pen-mark moment? What happened? How did it make you feel?

6. True or False (your opinion of these statements):

_____ Impersonating perfection stems from insecurities about our abilities.

_____ Impersonating perfection causes us to fall into the comparison trap with others.

_____ Impersonating perfection brings hollow satisfaction in the end.

Behind Your Eyes

1. If you are married, in what ways do you experience the perfect wife syndrome in your life?

2. If you are single, why is it important to realize that portraying perfectionism in a relationship is not helpful? How can that knowledge help you in your relationships with others?

3. If you have children, in what ways do you experience the perfect mom syndrome in your life?

4. In this chapter, you read about my friend Tiffany's struggle with perfection, which led to an eating disorder. Do you see how one could be a catalyst for the other? Consider

her statement: "I have learned that peace comes from my relationship with Christ, not my weight, my clothing size, what car I drive, or how many church functions I attend." How does this statement play out for you in your life? What areas of perfection do you struggle with the most?

Challenge Question

Search your heart. Is it more important for you to be seen as perfect in a certain area . . . or seen as real?

Getting Real

Are you ready to hear the truth? Ask a trusted friend, "Do people see me as someone who tries to be perfect or as someone who is real?" Be ready to hear the truth about yourself through their eyes.

Heavenly Father, thank You for seeing us from the inside out.
Thank You for desiring a relationship with Your daughters
that is based on love and grace rather than perfectionism.
May we, through Your power, break free
from the trap of trying to be perfect.
May we replace our old efforts with
newer, more spiritually minded ones.
In Jesus' name. Amen.

three MS. CONFIDENCE

Reality Check

Confidence is something that seems to exude from certain people. Many times we are led to believe that someone is confident merely by the facade of strength and independence that she wears. In reality, there is often a huge difference in what is portrayed on the outside and what is really going on inside someone's heart. Ms. Confidence wants you to buy into her confident charade while she may be one of the most insecure people to ever walk into a room. But she keeps the truth of the matter very close to the vest so that her confident cover will never be blown. This chapter exposes the truth about who qualifies as a truly confident woman.

Challenge Verse

Such confidence as this is ours through Christ before God.
—2 Corinthians 3:4

Truth Talk

1. What does having confidence mean to you?

2. How do you feel when you are around someone who portrays confidence? Why?

3. Is there a difference between true confidence and impersonated confidence? What is it?

4. To what degree does fear of rejection play into Ms. Confidence's role-playing? Why?

5. Ask yourself the following questions posed in this chapter, and give your own thoughts about them.

Would a confident woman share her body openly with others, expose it freely, and use it to her advantage?

_____

Why or why not?

_____

Would a truly confident woman be so self-assured that she would have no real emotional need for others?

_____

Why or why not?

_____

6. On pages 55–56, I give some definitions of a new perspective on confidence. Write your own definitions of these words, personalizing them for you in your circumstances.

Fearless: _____

Strong: _____

Empowered: _____

Independent: _____

Emotionally Healthy: _____

Accomplished: _____

Behind Your Eyes

1. Meditate on the truth that we really need only God. Do

you believe this to be true? Have you lived your life feeling as if you needed others to survive?

2. Has the fact that you really need only God in this life ever been tested in your own life? What happened, and how did God show Himself to be sufficient?

3. A portion of the Paula Rinehart quote on page 46 says, "You can't shut down on the inside without quelling the very passion that makes the journey worthwhile." Can you relate to this thought? How?

Challenge Question

Be completely introspective. Is it hard for you to admit your vulnerabilities to others? To God? Why?

Getting Real

Get a piece of paper and divide it into two columns. On one side write what it will cost you emotionally to admit your vulnerabilities. (Be specific.) On the other side write what it will cost you emotionally to deny your vulnerabilities. Look at both lists . . . is the price worth it?

Dear Lord, we admit that as capable as we may be, we cannot be truly confident without the power of the Holy Spirit in our lives . . . leading us and directing us in our everyday circumstances. Our desire is that we begin to be transparent before You and those around us, admitting our vulnerabilities and helping others feel the freedom to, in turn, get real.
In Jesus' name. Amen.

four MS. HAPPINESS

Reality Check

Is what you see always what you get with people you encounter? Not necessarily. But it is certainly something that Ms. Happiness wants you to think about her. She tries tactics such as quick thrills, temporary pleasures, and indulgences to find true happiness, looking for it in outside relationships and even within herself. Yet all the sources that she seeks never really provide her lasting joy. Quite often, the smile she wears on the outside does not match the heartfelt hurt she feels on the inside. But still she wants you to think she is blissfully happy! This chapter debunks the myths about happiness, presenting the truth about the source of joy.

Challenge Verse

You have made known to me the path of life; you will fill me with joy in your presence, with eternal pleasures at your right hand. —Psalm 16:11

Truth Talk

1. Why do you think we see happiness as the holy grail in life?

2. Do you agree that our standards for happiness are not really all that high most of the time? Why do you think this is?

3. Recall the avenues of Ms. Happiness in seeking happiness:

You can make _____ happy (page 62).

_____ you _____ can make you happy (page 63).

_____ you _____ or _____ can make you happy (page 65).

Which of these statements has been true or is currently true for you in your life? Why?

4. A portion of the Robert E. Quinn quote on page 62 says, "It is our hypocrisy and self-focus that drains us." Do you agree or disagree? Why is this so detrimental to our happiness and fulfillment in life?

5. What do you think about the United States, with its lavish lifestyles in relation to other much less fortunate countries, deemed less happy than others? Is this a coincidence, or is there a correlation?

6. Do you see the value in digging to find the *source* of joy? Why is this so important?

7. This chapter portrays happiness as a surface condition and joy as a deeply rooted condition. Think of some other things that are surface versus deeply rooted. Which greater benefit and why?

Behind Your Eyes

1. Do you believe that what you see is truly what you get as it relates to Ms. Happiness? Is what others see in you truly what they are getting when they really get to know you?

2. Consider the life of Solomon (Eccl. 2). Can you relate to his struggles? In what way(s)?

3. Look back at the verses on pages 72–73. Which of these relates best to your life? Why? Write it down and memorize it.

Challenge Question

Honestly . . . do you have true joy? If not, what is standing in your way of receiving it?

Getting Real

Think about a person you know who emulates true joy. If possible, get in touch with that person and ask him or her what is the source of that joy. If not, think of reasons why others have such joy, and pray for those things to be true in your life as well.

*Father God, we are women who desire
to find joy, fulfillment, and peace in life.
We know that only You can provide these things.
But we admit we have sought other sources
to make us happy, and they have only brought us
very temporary feelings of fulfillment.
You are our joy, and we seek You as our only way to be
the happy women we want to be.
In Jesus' name. Amen.*

five MS. SPIRITUALITY

Reality Check

Oh, the games Ms. Spirituality plays! Her desire to portray a deeply spiritual person often stifles her from the depth she craves, yet her spiritual standing is more important to her than her desire to get real. So she keeps on pretending. Ms. Spirituality is far more caught up in her rituals than her relationship with Christ, and just like the other impersonated roles that have gone before her, much of her time, energy, and resources are wrapped up in keeping up the charade. This role is the most dangerous role to impersonate, yet its prevalence is widespread. This chapter takes an honest look at what it means to be truly spiritual.

Challenge Verse

To be spiritually minded is life and peace. —Romans 8:6 NKJV

Truth Talk

1. Reread Luke 8:42–48 and the story of the woman who was bleeding: "When the woman realized that she couldn't remain hidden, she knelt trembling before him" (v. 47 MSG). (If

you have Internet access, you can go to www.biblegateway.com to read the story in *The Message* rendering.) Why do you think it was important for this woman to expose her vulnerabilities to Jesus and others that day?

2. Why is being spiritually transparent so important? Why is the danger so high to keep impersonating spirituality without actually embodying it?

3. On page 78, some attributes of Ms. Spirituality are listed. What is the difference between Ms. Spirituality and a truly spiritual woman in relation to those attributes?

4. Define *spirituality*. How does society define it? How do your definition and society's definition differ if they do?

5. Do you believe you can be truly spiritual without putting forth some "spiritual muscle" (James 1:22)? What specific actions are required for that?

6. How can the attitude of people like the man at church on page 85 help our churches get real? How would the opposite attitude hinder that kind of authenticity?

7. True or False: a person who is truly spiritual exudes the spirit of God. Why does this trump our manufactured spirituality?

Behind Your Eyes

1. Define *faith* in a personal way . . . as it relates to your life.

2. "Praise the LORD, O my soul, and forget not all his benefits" (Ps. 103:2). What are some of the benefits of God in your life or in the lives of those whom you believe to be truly spiritual? Be specific.

3. Meditate on Galatians 5:22–23 and the fruit of the Spirit. Which is easiest for you to live out? Which is hardest? Why do you think that is?

Challenge Question

Now we're really getting personal. Are you trading your reputation for repentance? Do you need to get spiritually real?

Getting Real

Choose a person in the Bible with a spiritual quality you admire. Study about him or her in the Word, find biblical commentaries on that person or person's story, and determine where that quality came from.

Lord, more than anything else, we need to go deeper with You.
We need to love You more, serve You more,
crave You more, and honor You more.
With all of our hearts we want to know You.
Give us spiritual eyes to see the truth about our spiritual
condition. Help us to see the sneaky patterns of Satan and
his tactics to keep us busy in Your name instead of spending
our lives as living sacrifices, holy and acceptable to You.
In Jesus' name. Amen.

six COSMETICS FOR THE SOUL

Reality Check

The truth is that many of us waste time trying to cover up for things we don't like about ourselves, seeking to hide our pain. Although the original cover-up conspiracy started in the garden so long ago, we continue in that same rat race as we scurry around trying to conceal broken hearts and souls. Down deep inside, we as women know the truth: we have become experts at concealing things that we feel we need to keep hidden. Otherwise, we fear we may not be accepted or loved. This chapter shows how the concealment of our souls robs us of meaningful interactions with people.

Challenge Verse

You open your hand and satisfy the desires of every living thing. —Psalm 145:16

Truth Talk

1. Define *cosmetics for the soul*. What does that phrase mean to you?

2. What is the correlation between concealing our souls and impersonating the women we want to be?

3. Pages 101–02 talk about the original cover-up conspiracy of Adam and Eve in the garden. How do their actions that day relate to what we do to stay free from exposure?

4. What is society's role in our desire to stay hidden from God?

5. Does Satan also play a role in that desire?

6. What role have our own personal choices played?

7. Where does true satisfaction in life come from? How could finding true satisfaction in life help us stop our impersonations for good?

Behind Your Eyes

1. Recall a time when emotional identity theft happened to you. Who or what played the biggest role in making you feel robbed of your identity?

2. Have you ever felt as though you got the short end of the stick in life? Recall the incident or experience and tell how that had an influence on the decisions you made from that point forward.

3. Consider Jeremiah 49:10. In this verse, the Lord refers to Esau and how He will deal with him and his descendants, the wicked Edomites, when He says, "I will uncover his hiding places, so that he cannot conceal himself." Does this verse comfort you, allowing you to rest in the fact that you can be your true self with God, or does it frighten you, making you feel nervous to be exposed before Him? Why?

Challenge Question

Pause long enough to give this question some thought. Are you currently satisfied or dissatisfied with your life? Why do you think that is? If you are satisfied, how do you think you can maintain that? If you are dissatisfied, how can you change it?

Getting Real

Write down the words *needy*, *broken*, and *hurt*. Make a list next to each word. Identify the ways you are needy. Why are or were you broken? How you have been hurt? One by one surrender those needs, broken places, and hurts over to Him. Pray with your palms up, openly exposing them to Jesus and allowing Him to take them and discard them from your soul forever.

> *Heavenly Father, it is good to be open with You.*
> *It is so hard to continue to carry burdens and hurts,*
> *trying so hard to conceal them from others. We are tired*
> *of trying. Take our needy hearts and broken souls*
> *in Your strong hands and restore them to health.*
> *For some of us, it may be the first time we have ever*
> *been well. For others of us, it's been a long time coming.*
> *But either way, be our Jehovah Rapha, the One who heals.*
> *In Jesus' name. Amen.*

seven THE FEELINGS WE CONCEAL

Reality Check
It's hard for all of us at times to take a long, hard look in the mirror. When we do, we often don't like what we see, preferring to keep our *ugly* hidden. And I'm not talking about our physical looks. What I am talking about goes so much deeper. It is painful to admit that we can have strong feelings of insecurity, jealousy, loneliness, and fear . . . often to the point of actions resulting from them. We find out pretty early in life that pretending is a great way to keep these feelings concealed from others and even from ourselves. This chapter gets to the core of the feelings we are experiencing that we prefer to keep hidden.

Challenge Verse
He searches the sources of the rivers and brings hidden things to light. —Job 28:11

Truth Talk
1. Read the account of Joseph and his brothers in Genesis 37. What was the driving force behind the brothers' actions? How did they cover up for it?

2. Which of the four qualities on pages 118–19 of fantastic friends Jonathan and David do you most crave in a friendship? If you have this type of friendship with someone already, which of these qualities do you have?

3. Why is jealousy such a dangerous emotion?

4. In the words of the Julie Roberts song, "I'm already lonely, I might as well be lonely alone," there is a strong message in a short phrase. What is it? How can a person be lonely if she is in a crowd of people?

5. What seven-letter word that I admitted to, dealing with my fear of flying, is quite often behind many of our fears (page 126)? Why is this such a powerful emotion?

Behind Your Eyes

1. Both big and small, what types of things in your life have you tried to conceal?

Small _____ Big _____

_____ _____

_____ _____

2. How much of your life have you spent trying to conceal things from others? Circle one of the following:

None   Very little   Some   A lot   Most of it

Did it work? Why won't it last long-term?

3. How has insecurity manifested itself in your life? Do others see you as insecure, or do you think you hide it well?

4. Have you ever felt the brunt of another woman's jealousy toward you? Did it cause you to shy away from making female friends?

5. In what ways have you experienced loneliness in your life? What have you done both negatively and positively to remedy it?

6. What are you most afraid of? What was the catalyst for your fear?

Challenge Question
Dig deep. What is the most painful feeling for you to conceal? Why?

Getting Real
Write a letter to someone you have hurt out of your feelings of insecurity, jealousy, loneliness, or fear. Pray over the letter, and ask God what you should do with it. If you feel led to do so, send it to that person, and ask God to help him or her to receive it with an open and loving spirit.

Jesus, we acknowledge that You are able to
heal every feeling of insecurity, jealousy, loneliness, or fear.
We know that so many times we lash out in anger,
thinking we are mad at someone, yet it is really
our own underlying insecurities
and fears that bring that emotion out in us.
Be our bridge to healing over the troubled waters of our lives.
We trust You with our feelings and emotions,
no matter how fragile they are.
In Jesus' name. Amen.

eight WE ARE COMPLETELY LOVED AND ACCEPTED COMPLETELY

Reality Check

It is no secret to any of us that we long to feel loved. We all crave acceptance. But searching for it in the things of this world certainly has let us down many times. In a relationship with Jesus Christ, we can enjoy true love without conditions or pretense. When we become His child, we no longer have to question our heritage, no matter how unsteady our earthly relationships may be. This chapter explores God's love and acceptance of us and compares them to the conditional standards set by the world.

Challenge Verse

How great is the love the Father has lavished on us, that we should be called children of God! And that is what we are!
—1 John 3:1

Truth Talk

1. Why is God's love for us so hard to comprehend?

2. In what way(s) have you felt the limitations of earthly love? How does it contrast to God's love?

3. The Gospels (Matt. 27; Mark 14–15; Luke 22–23; John 18–19) detail the death of Jesus Christ on the cross. Read one or all of these passages and describe in writing how He showed you love by dying on the cross for your sins. Attach specific actions to it (e.g., He was spat upon, suffered rejection).

4. On page 137, Brennan Manning is quoted about his own personal experience with God's love in a seminary chapel. What does he mean when he describes God's love as a storm? Can you relate?

5. How does the story about the Skittles relate to God's acceptance of you?

6. Reread the verses listed on page 141. Has God convinced you yet that He has adopted you as His child and accepts you completely? If not, what are some things that could be blocking that?

Behind Your Eyes

1. What example(s) in your life has convinced you that we aren't very good at loving others? On a scale of 1 to 10 (1 being "not hurt at all" and 10 being "very deeply hurt"), how much did it hurt you and cause you to question love?

1   2   3   4   5   6   7   8   9   10

2. In what sources have you sought to find love?
Internet _____   Shopping _____
Religion _____   Physical relationships _____
Food _____   Other _____

3. The quote by Robert Frost on page 135 says, "Love is an irresistible desire to be irresistibly desired." Do you feel

irresistibly desired by God? Do you think He feels equally desired by you? Why or why not?

4. Write down in detail a time when God paused to show you how much He cared about you through a unique circumstance. How did it make you feel?

Challenge Question

When you really get down to it, do you most need to know that you are completely loved by God or accepted completely? Which one, or why both? How much of your life has been spent seeking love or acceptance?

Getting Real

Write a love letter to God, saying whatever is on your heart. Then write a love letter to you from God.

Oh, great Lover of our souls, thank You for
Your unending, perfect love.
What a gift it is to be loved by You.
Thank You for adopting us into Your family
and giving us a rich inheritance of mercy and grace.
It is a privilege to call You Abba, Father. As we
draw near to You today, we ask that You draw near to us.
Help us to get to know You as our Dad.
In Jesus' name. Amen.

nine WE ARE COMPLETELY FLAWED YET FORGIVEN COMPLETELY

Reality Check

Most of us will readily agree that we are flawed in some way. We don't have to look far to find things about ourselves that we would like to change or don't like. But knowing that we are flawed doesn't have to result in self-loathing. Being flawed in God's big picture of things is an important aspect of His forgiveness of us. It is important for us to recognize that though we are all flawed, we are all equally forgiven by the mercy and grace of Jesus Christ and His death for us on the cross. This chapter encourages us to see our flaws for what they are and what they mean to our redemption.

Challenge Verse

In him we have redemption through his blood, the forgiveness of sins, in accordance with the riches of God's grace. —Ephesians 1:7

Truth Talk

1. Why are absolute words such as *always*, *completely*, *totally*, and *fully* so important to our understanding of forgiveness?

2. How does being flawed play into our relationship with God? Is it a positive thing or a negative thing?

3. What do the words *sin nature* mean to you?

4. What is the beauty in letting oneself be seen (both to others and to ourselves) as perfectly imperfect?

5. Does being flawed mean that we are bad or terrible? Why do we often think it does?

6. Do you believe this statement is true? "We don't fully understand God's forgiveness because forgiveness by others so often eludes us on this earth." What is so difficult about this?

7. Why are the specific details in Psalm 103:12 so important to the principle of forgiveness? (Hint: listen to Casting Crowns' song "East to West.")

Behind Your Eyes

1. What most frustrates you about forgiveness? What most frees you about it?

2. Do you relate to Paul's struggle with his flesh that he writes about in the book of Romans? (Refer to pages 154–55.) In what way(s)? What emotions do you think he was feeling when he wrote about it?

3. What is blocking you from feeling God's forgiveness? What is blocking you from forgiving someone else . . . or even yourself?

Challenge Question

In your heart of hearts, do you think God is ready and willing to forgive you? Honestly . . . will you let Him?

Getting Real

Commit to pray every day for the next five days, three minutes of solid prayer for someone who has hurt you. Pray for her by name. Pray that you will be able to forgive her, pray for her health, pray for her family, and pray for her salvation and spiritual condition. Ask God if there is someone from whom you need to ask forgiveness. Pray about the best way to approach that person and for the strength to do so.

Lord, You are the great Restorer of lives.
We ask You today by Your Holy Spirit to convict
and convince us of those we need to forgive
or those who may need to forgive us.
Help us to be spiritually strong so that we can
allow ourselves the permission to be flawed.
Remind us that while it is in our nature to be sinful,
it is in Your nature to be good and kind and merciful.
We are in desperate need of Your
forgiveness today . . . and every day.
In Jesus' name. Amen.

ten THE TRUTH HEALS

Reality Check

We start and end the book talking about the same truth. But while initially we discussed how truth and authenticity sometimes hurt, we now discover how that same truth can be the healing agent we need to start truly living. In the end, the healing power of the Truth is what keeps us willing to stay real and open with God, others, and ourselves about our flaws, failures, and fears. When we recognize who we are, own our missteps from the past, and resolve to be the *me* God created each of us to be, we can and will experience the freeing power of the Truth. This chapter implores us to seek the Truth, not temporary salves or quick fixes, to once and for all heal our souls.

Challenge Verse

You will know the truth, and the truth will set you free.
—John 8:32

Truth Talk

1. How can the truth hurt and heal at the same time?

2. How can resolving to be you and no one else help determine the fate of your role-playing in the future?

3. Do you see the difference between a soothing balm and a healing balm? What is it? Write about a time when you experienced either or both.

4. Which of the three main truths in this chapter do you struggle with the most (recognition, admission, or resolution)? Why?

5. On pages 176–77, how a frustrated dieter often handles one caloric mistake is compared to our owning our mistakes from the past. Do you find yourself in this example as it relates to making mistakes in your daily life? In what way(s)?

Behind Your Eyes

1. Do you feel that you know the truth about yourself? Has that knowledge helped free you on some level? Why or why not?

2. Think about a time when you felt set up by someone you knew or trusted who didn't portray truth to you. Why was this so memorable to you?

3. How did you view or how do you currently see God in His creation of you? As a master craftsman or as having an "oops!" moment? If you need to, how can you change your perspective in this regard?

4. Can you truly say that you own your mistakes from the past? Can you separate owning and acknowledging them from punishing yourself for them? Why or why not?

5. Look back over the verses on pages 190–91 Insert your name before each verse and take the time to slowly drink in each truth. What is the link between all of them?

Challenge Question

It's truth time. Is your soul truly set free? Is the truth behind your eyes the same as what others see?

Getting Real

Just as I did on pages 187–89 write down your own personal reflections of things in your life that are positive but haven't been able to fix your broken places. After you do, tell Jesus just how much you love and appreciate Him for being the only One who can.

Holy God, we lay our burdens down at the foot of the cross,
knowing that You are the One and
only Truth capable of setting us free.
We expose our broken places before You,
for our souls long to be mended.
Pick up the pieces of our hearts that need repair,
and pour Your healing balm over them. We love You.
We adore You. We seek Your truth and the freedom it brings.
In Jesus' name. Amen.

NOTES

one The Truth Hurts

1. John Eldredge, *The Sacred Romance* (Nashville: Thomas Nelson, Inc., 2001), 9. Reprinted by permission. All rights reserved.

three Ms. Confidence

1. Paula Rinehart, *Strong Women, Soft Hearts* (Nashville: Thomas Nelson, Inc., 2005), 104–05. Reprinted by permission. All rights reserved.
2. Mary K. Moore and Rose Martelli, "10 Habits of Confident Women," *Redbook*, www.redbookmag.com/your/confident-women-yl, accessed 9 January 2008.

four Ms. Happiness

1. Amy Lowell, *Sword Blades and Poppy Seed* (Kila, MT: Kessinger Publishing, 2004).
2. Robert E. Quinn, *Building the Bridge as You Walk on It: A Guide for Leading Change* (New York: Jossey-Bass, 2004).
3. "It Is Well with My Soul," words by Horatio G. Spafford, music by Philip P. Bliss, © 1873, 1876.
4. Crystal Boyd, *Midnight Muse* ©2000 by Crystal Boyd; www.crystalboyd.com.
5. R. C. Kessler, W. T. Chiu, O. Demler, E. E. Walters, "Prevalence, Severity, and Comorbidity of twelve-month DSM-IV disorders," National Comorbidity Survey Replication (NCS-R). Archives of *General Psychiatry*, 2005 June; 62(6):617–27. Can be accessed at www.nimh.nih.gov/health/publications/the-numbers-count-mental-disorders-in-america.shtml#KesslerPrevalence.
6. "Depression," www.fda.gov/womens/getthefacts/depression.html, accessed 9 January 2008.
7. Mayo Clinic Staff, "Depression in Women: Understanding the Gender Gap," Mayo Foundation for Medical Education and Research, 20 September 2006, www.mayoclinic.com/health/depression/MH00035, accessed 9 January 2008.
8. L. Camfield, K. Choudhury, and J. Devine, "Relationships, Happiness, and Well-Being: Insights from Bangladesh," ESRC Research Group on Wellbeing in Developing Countries, March 2006. Can be accessed at

www.bath.ac.uk/econ-dev/wellbeing/research/
workingpaperpdf/wed14.pdf.

9. Anne Frank, *The Diary of a Young Girl* (New York: Bantam, 1993).

10. *The Weight of Glory* by C. S. Lewis copyright © C. S. Lewis Pte. Ltd. 1949. Extract reprinted by permission.

11. "I've Got the Joy, Joy, Joy, Joy" (sometimes titled simply "I've Got the Joy") is a popular contemporary Christian-based song often sung around a campfire or during scouting events. It is often included in gospel music and a cappella concerts and song books. The origin of the words and music is unknown.

five Ms. Spirituality

1. Definition of spirituality as found on www.religioustolerance.org/gl_s1.htm, accessed 9 January 2008. Used by permission of www.religioustolerance.org.

2. "Stained Glass Masquerade" by Mark Hall and Nichole Nordeman. Copyright © 2005 Birdwing Music (ASCAP), Club Zoo Music (BMI), SWECS Music (BMI), Birdboy Songs (ASCAP), My Refuge Music (BMI), admin. by EMI CMG Publishing. All rights reserved. Used by permission.

3. Ravi Zacharias, *Recapture the Wonder* (Nashville: Thomas Nelson, Inc., 2001), 78. Reprinted by permission. All rights reserved.

4. Erwin McManus, *Soul Cravings* (Nashville: Thomas Nelson, Inc., 2006), Destiny Entry #22: Standardized Testing. Reprinted by permission. All rights reserved.

5. Ibid.

six Cosmetics for the Soul

1. Jennifer White, "In Pursuit of Big Dreams, Don't Let Dissatisfaction Obscure Life's Wonders," *Kansas City Business Journal*, 19 January 2001.

2. Ibid.

seven The Feelings We Conceal

1. Story used by permission of Ron Hutchcraft, www.hutchcraft.com. Used by permission.

2. Lisa Bevere, *Fight Like a Girl: The Power of Being a Woman* (New York: FaithWords, a division of Time Warner Books, 2006).

3. Ibid.

4. Commentary on 1 Samuel 18:1, *New Living Translation*, copyright

©1996. Used by permission of Tyndale House Publishers, Inc., Wheaton, IL 60189 USA. All rights reserved.

5. "Men and Mascara," written by Marv Green, Chris Lindsey, Hillary Lindsey, and Aimee Mayo. © 2006 Warner-Tamerlane Publishing Corp. (BMI); BMG Songs, Inc./Magic Farming Music, admin. by BMG Songs, Inc. (ASCAP); Raylene Music, admin. by BPJ Administration (ASCAP); Little Blue Typewriter Music, admin. by BPJ Administration (BMI). All rights reserved.

6. Judy Foreman, "Loneliness Can Be the Death of the US," *Boston Globe*, 22 April 1996.

7. "Loneliness" survey, www.efmoody.com/miscellaneous/ loneliness.html, accessed 9 January 2008.

8. Eric Hoffer, "Thoughts of Eric Hoffer, Including 'Absolute Faith Corrupts Absolutely,'" *The New York Times Magazine*, 25 April 1971, 55.

9. Beth Moore, *Further Still* (Nashville: Broadman & Holman, 2004), 29.

eight We Are Completely Loved and Accepted Completely

1. Robert McGee, *The Search for Significance* (Nashville: Thomas Nelson, Inc., 2003).

2. Justin Hutchins, "What Is It That I Love?" www.lovepoemsandquotes.com/LoveQuote07.html, accessed 9 January 2008.

3. "Searching for Love (It's Real)," written by BeBe Winans and Angie Winans ©1991. BMI Blackwood Music, Inc.

4. Brennan Manning, *Above All* (Nashville: Thomas Nelson, Inc., 2003), 97–98. Reprinted by permission. All rights reserved.

5. "Clean Before My Lord," Honeytree © 1976 Word Music, LLC. All rights reserved. Used by permission.

nine We Are Completely Flawed yet Forgiven Completely

1. Commentary from Luke 23, *New Living Translation*, copyright ©1996. Used by permission of Tyndale House Publishers, Inc., Wheaton, IL 60189 USA. All rights reserved.

ten The Truth Heals

1. "There Is a Balm in Gilead," African American spiritual, words and music.

2. Brenda Hunter, *My God, Do You Love Me? A Woman's Conversations with God* (Colorado Springs: WaterBrook Press, 1984), 1–2.